The**Personality**Code

The **Personality** Code

Unlock the Secret to Understanding

Your Boss, Your Colleagues, Your

Friends . . . and Yourself

Travis Bradberry

G. P. Putnam's Sons

a member of Penguin Group (USA) Inc., New York

G. P. PUTNAM'S SONS
Publishers Since 1838
Published by the Penguin Group
Penguin Group (USA) Inc., 375 Hudson Street, New York, New York 10014, USA •
Penguin Group (Canada), 90 Eglinton Avenue East, Suite 700, Toronto, Ontario M4P 2Y3,
Canada (a division of Pearson Penguin Canada Inc.) • Penguin Books Ltd, 80 Strand, London WC2R 0RL,
England • Penguin Ireland, 25 St Stephen's Green, Dublin 2, Ireland (a division of Penguin Books Ltd) •
Penguin Group (Australia), 250 Camberwell Road, Camberwell, Victoria 3124, Australia (a division of
Pearson Australia Group Pty Ltd) • Penguin Books India Pvt Ltd, 11 Community Centre, Panchsheel Park,
New Delhi–110 017, India • Penguin Group (NZ), 67 Apollo Drive, Rosedale, North Shore 0745,
Auckland, New Zealand (a division of Pearson New Zealand Ltd) • Penguin Books
(South Africa) (Pty) Ltd, 24 Sturdee Avenue, Rosebank, Johannesburg 2196, South Africa

Penguin Books Ltd, Registered Offices: 80 Strand, London WC2R 0RL, England

Library of Congress Cataloging-in-Publication Data

Bradberry, Travis.
The personality code : unlock the secret to understanding your boss, your colleagues,
your friends . . . and yourself / Travis Bradberry.
p.   cm.
Includes bibliographical references and index.
ISBN-13: 978-0-399-15411-9
1. Personality. I. Title.
BF698.B659   2007   2007000537
155.2—dc22

Printed in the United States of America
1 3 5 7 9 10 8 6 4 2

BOOK DESIGN BY NICOLE LAROCHE

Nothing in this book is intended as an express or implied warranty of the suitability or fitness of any product,
service, or design. Readers wishing to use a product, service, or design discussed in this book should first consult
a specialist or professional to ensure suitability and fitness for their particular lifestyle and environmental needs.

While the author has made every effort to provide accurate telephone numbers and Internet addresses at the
time of publication, neither the publisher nor the author assumes any responsibility for errors, or for changes
that occur after publication. Further, the publisher does not have any control over and does not assume any
responsibility for author or third-party websites or their content.

To the Smarties

Contents

Introduction: Separated at Birth

IN LATE NOVEMBER 1958, newborn identical twin boys were delivered to an orphanage on the southernmost island of Japan. The boys' mother, unwed and abandoned by their father, had committed suicide upon their birth. She couldn't bear the intense shame placed on women who raised children alone. A few months later, the twins were discovered by a sergeant from the U.S. Air Force named Claude Patterson, who was stationed in Japan. Claude and his wife had high hopes of adopting a child they could bring back home to the United States. The Pattersons fell in love with both boys and requested to adopt the pair. To their dismay, the orphanage offered just one boy, with the explanation that the older brother was already spoken for. Forced with the choice of dividing the twins or looking elsewhere, the Pattersons chose to adopt the younger twin. They raised him in rural Kansas and gave him an American name, Tom. The older twin was also adopted by a couple from the United States, who raised him in New Jersey and named him Steve. For the next forty years, Tom and Steve lived separate lives, each unaware that his identical twin was just six states away.

Both boys learned growing up that they were one half of an identical pair, but neither family knew anything of the other twin's whereabouts. For most of their lives, the twins' attempts at locating each other were futile, as the orphanage in Japan was destroyed by a fire shortly after they left the country. Their paths finally crossed on the last day of June 1999. Earlier that year, Steve discovered, through searchable adoption databases on the Internet, that his twin brother was adopted in 1958 by someone with the first name Claude and a last name of Patterson, Peterson, or Paulson. Steve e-mailed everyone in the adoption database who matched this description, with no luck. So he sent out hundreds of letters—one to every Claude Patterson, Peterson, and Paulson he could find an address for—seeking information on a twin adopted in southern Japan in 1958. One of these letters ended up in the hands of retired Air Force sergeant Claude Patterson, who was still living in rural Kansas, just a short drive from his son, Tom. When Claude read the handwritten letter, he could scarcely believe his eyes. Could this really be the same boy he was forced to leave behind in the orphanage more than forty years earlier? He had to find out. He drove straight to his son's house, and they called the number given in the letter. Less than a week later, Tom and Steve stood face-to-face in the middle of terminal D at the airport in Philadelphia.

When they approached each other for the first time that day, the two buff men in red sweatshirts paused silently for a moment to size each other up. Seeing their spitting image standing in front of them was almost too much for the hulking, identical figures to bear. "I literally could not believe he looked exactly like me," Steve recalls, "but when I did see him, I—I was in awe. I was just totally in awe about it. Even if you look at our teeth, I have a separation in the exact same place that he does. It's . . . it's just amazing how much he looks like me. It's like looking into a mirror."

The twins spent the next four days together, trying desperately to catch up on forty years of separation. It didn't take long for them to discover they had far more in common than their looks. Both brought the same restless intensity to the conversation—head cocked to the left, a stiff upper body, and legs that bounced along attentively with each word spoken. Despite being raised in contrasting environments—Tom in a Christian household in small-town Kansas, and Steve as a Buddhist in a metropolitan borough of New Jersey—their lives had followed starkly similar paths. Both men had married Caucasian women, had two children, and had given their firstborn a Japanese name and their second child an American name. They found unusual similarities in everything, from how fast they talk to how they like to organize the sock drawer. These similarities are compelling, yet it's tempting to dismiss them as uncanny coincidences. It was when their discussion turned to careers that Tom and Steve knew there was something bigger at play. Like many other boys growing up, both were fanatical about sports. Though each was exposed to a myriad of athletics, bodybuilding so captured their interest that it led to an identical choice in profession—each owned and operated a gym in his hometown. But why did they choose to own a gym as their career? Both men delighted in the virtue of keeping the body physically fit, and possessed the remarkable amount of discipline required to maintain a statuesque physique. More important, they were both drawn by the opportunity to help others do the same.

Life is filled with choices. There are an infinite number of junctures on the road that can lead two people—even genetically identical twins—

on disparate paths. Tom and Steve didn't try to be the same; they weren't even raised in similar homes. So what was it that kept them headed in the same direction? The twins share an identical personality—the single enigmatic element of the mind that is so central to who we are that it led two men to get out of bed in the morning carrying the same motivations, pursue the same interests, choose the identical profession, and ultimately land in the same place in life.

The Personality Code is a book that explores the vital role of personality in who we are today and what we become tomorrow.

The TalentSmart Study

The impetus for this book surfaced more than a decade ago, in the form of a perplexing question batted around among a group of industrial psychologists: "Is there a universal characteristic that makes people successful?" With no answer in sight, this conundrum needled our curiosity. We decided to launch a study to find out. We assembled a team of statisticians, programmers, administrators, and psychologists to execute a global search for the universal source of talent. Aptly named the TalentSmart study, this quest operated outside the confines of an underlying theory—any preconceived notions as to what produces success would only muddy the waters. TalentSmart took a broad brush and measured the scope of people's skills, motivations, and opinions. We observed their behavior at work and at home. And, perhaps more important, we noted the choices people made and measured the results that followed. An overarching determinant of success, should it exist, could only be found by separating the actions that get results from those that are inconsequential or even harmful.

The TalentSmart study grew rapidly and by the time it was complete we had profiled people on every inhabited continent. This enormous database contains millions of pieces of information that represent the input of more than 500,000 people in ninety-four countries. (See Appendix B for details of the study sample.) At the heart of *The Personality Code* are the discoveries from this effort. And, yes, the answer to our question ultimately surfaced, but not before we had stumbled upon two revelations that fly in the face of what people have been told their entire lives will make them successful: (1) your personality sets your direction in life, and (2) the greater your self-awareness, the more able you are to use personality to achieve your fullest potential.

Character Is Destiny

In our homes, schools, and the workplace we're encouraged to pull ourselves up by our bootstraps and be the person we wish to become. Success, we're told, is a matter of choice. The incredible flaw in this well-intended advice? We actually have very little say in the matter. Like a massive boulder tearing down a hillside, our destiny is set in motion by our personality—a set of behavior traits we all possess in varying degrees. Like the tendency toward introversion or extraversion, these traits influence how we think, how we feel, and ultimately what we do. Each of us has a personality profile that reflects our own unique blend of the personality traits, and is produced by hardwired paths for thinking in the brain. By the time we reach adulthood, these paths are fixed. They serve as the conduits by which our brains think, the mental funnels through which our choices must flow. Personality is a collection of our motivations, needs, and preferences that serves as a blueprint to our strengths and weaknesses—each individual's "code," as it were.

Steve Tazumi and Tom Patterson didn't choose to take identical paths in life; they simply followed their hearts. These men pursued the activities that held their interest, enjoyed the opportunities that made good use of their talents, and fell in love with someone who made them feel complete. Before they met, each man considered himself the master of his own destiny. So it was incredibly unnerving at age forty for each to meet his clone living the same life six states away. Steve's and Tom's matching lives were driven by matching personalities, which is an unusual occurrence, even for identical twins. The personality traits measured by the TalentSmart study yield more than 123,000 unique configurations. This means it's highly unlikely you'll ever bump into someone who shares your *exact* personality profile.

The brain is the most complicated organ in the human body, and there are a multitude of methods available for sizing up how people think and what makes them tick. We administered a myriad of tests in the TalentSmart study, to measure the variety of qualities that people bring to the table. We were surprised to see the degree to which personality traits influence so much of what people say and do each day. The real power in managing human behavior lies in the very code of our own personalities—it is the single artifact of the mind that is so pervasive that it is the key to

Personality is the essence of a person's character, revealed in predictable patterns of inclinations and behavior; a collection of our motivations, needs, and preferences that—once understood—provides a blueprint to our strengths and weaknesses.

developing self-awareness. Your personality profile is, to the greatest extent, who you are; it captures the essence of your motivations and preferences in life. Since your profile doesn't change, aligning your efforts with it is the only way you can use it to your advantage. Personality is the tool that can pave the way to success, or leave you inexplicably stuck.

The study of personality can be approached broadly with meaningful results. You don't need to squander valuable time fixating on the minute details of people's behavior to put your knowledge of personality to use. Through an extended series of statistical analyses, we were able to condense the 123,000 possible personality configurations into fourteen unique personality types. These types represent the fourteen kinds of people that can be discerned based on their fixed personalities. This book includes a pass code that lets you go online and take the IDISC™ personality profiler to discover your own type. You'll learn which of the fourteen personality profiles you are, and how you can make the most of this hard-coded determinant of human behavior.

We ignore our personality at our own peril, for it sets our direction in life with or without our support and understanding.

Self-Awareness Breeds Success

If personality is fixed, then what is the point of knowing it? To be honest, we scratched our heads over this one for a good while. Personality was not the blanket predictor of success the study was seeking. True, it dictates the bulk of our behavior, but we found that successful people come from a mixed bag of personalities—they represent each of the fourteen types equally. Top performers may not share the same personality profile, but they do have one critical thing in common: an acute sense of self-awareness. Self-awareness is not about discovering deep, dark secrets or unconscious motivations, but, rather, it comes from developing a straightforward and honest understanding of what makes you tick. People high in self-awareness are remarkably clear in their understanding of what they are capable of doing well, what will motivate and satisfy them, and which people and situations they should avoid. As self-awareness increases, people's satisfaction with life—defined as their ability to reach their goals at work and at home—skyrockets. In the workplace, 83% of those high in self-awareness are top performers. Likewise, just 2% of bottom performers are high in self-awareness. Why is this so? Those who understand their preferences and tendencies are far more likely to pursue the right opportunities, put their strengths to work, and get results. When we learn the ins and outs of our ingrained style for responding to challenges and opportunities, we discover the situations and people that will make us successful.

The need for self-awareness has never been greater. Guided by the mistaken notion that psychology deals exclusively with pathology, we assume that the only time to learn about ourselves is in the face of crisis. We embrace those things with which we're comfortable, and put on the blinders the moment something makes us uncomfortable. But it's really the whole picture that serves us. The more we understand the beauty and the blemishes, the more we can put them both to work to achieve our potential. Regardless of your current level of self-awareness, you can increase this critical skill by closely studying your profile, which is a blueprint for your behavior.

The Journey into Your Personality

The Personality Code is an invitation to explore the inner workings of your mind, and no exploration of personality is complete without an objective measure of your own personality profile. Unlike the participants in the TalentSmart study, you won't have to submit to hours of testing to learn a great deal about yourself. The years that TalentSmart spent number crunching through this worldwide database have produced the IDISC, an online test that reveals your personality profile in just fifteen minutes. In Chapter 3 you'll learn how to take the IDISC, which will run your responses against the 123,000 possible configurations to crack your personality code. Your results reveal which of the fourteen personality types best describes you, as well as the significance of the unique variations seen in your personality profile. Testing yourself to discover your personality profile will deliver profound insights into your motivations, preferences, and the types of people with whom you'll have the most synergy personally and professionally. Some aspects of your personality profile will surprise you, and others will affirm things you already know about yourself. Since optimal performance is more about perspective than it is about effort, an objective measure of your personality is a critical first step to building the self-awareness you need to be your best.

Sometimes the biggest challenge is not in understanding yourself, but those around you. Much of *The Personality Code* is about deciphering people—with strategies you can employ at work and at home. Chapter 4 introduces each of the fourteen types of people in an easy-to-reference format. You'll gain a practical understanding of each type's defining characteristics, strengths, and challenges. In later chapters, you'll learn how to quickly size people up and respond to them based on their personality type. Stories help illustrate how personality has a profound impact on people's lives, and how understanding it helps you put it to good use. You can't change your personality profile, or the profiles of those around you, but you can use a positive understanding of personality to create more satisfying personal and professional relationships.

Our journey begins at the frontier of psychology and neuroscience—a place that provides startling new insights into the physical structure of personality inside the brain *and* its critical role in dictating what we do and say each day. These advances illuminate the very essence of human behavior.

For a behind-the-scenes look at the TalentSmart study and details on how the data from the study was analyzed, see Appendix B.

1: The Anatomy of Personality

A S JAMES PULLED the ax back high above his head, the muscles in his arms turned to rubber. He braced his shoulders to compensate for the weakness, and continued reaching back until the shaft was fully perpendicular to his outstretched body. A quick peek behind him sent a painful flash of sunlight off the gleaming blade and into his bifocals.

"We better move into the shade," James said, his eyes squinting while he gave his glasses a quick cleaning on his shirt.

Rick quit flinching, and bear-hugged the chopping block. He thrust back his shoulders as he stood, somehow managing to support the weight of the block with his wiry frame. Then he dropped his chin on top of it for balance as he waddled across the yard. James watched his best friend walking along with his head on the chopping block, and it reminded him of the medieval executions he had just read about in history class. James shivered.

The year was 1968—the heart of the Vietnam draft—and Rick's number had just been called. Underneath the patio awning of Rick's parents' single-story home, James once again swung the ax high above his head. The ax planted itself in the chopping block with the same dull thud it made when he chopped wood for his father. Rick snapped his hand back in shock, peering briefly at his missing thumb. The blood throbbed from the tiny stump with such force that it made him panic. He jammed his hand into the stack of towels set aside for the purpose and squeezed his wrist with the other hand to reduce the blood flow.

James was surprised how dark the blood was. It was nothing like what came out of his cuts during football. This train of thought made him queasy, so he reached for the hose to help his friend clean up. James crimped the hose to build pressure and sprayed the block with a powerful whoosh of water that sent the thumb flying. Rick's severed thumb skipped off the pavement and stopped against the fence. Rick didn't mind the rough treatment of his appendage; the draft wasn't taking boys with missing thumbs to the steamy jungles of Vietnam. The neighborhood had already lost three of its sons that summer, and Rick decided that losing his thumb was the only way he could—with certainty—spare his parents the pain of planning his funeral. He picked his thumb up and stuffed it in his pocket like he might his car keys or a pack of gum. No need to put the appendage on ice. He didn't want any doctor stitching it back on to ruin his plan. The boys buried the thumb in a planter and ran down the street to find Rick's parents and tell them about the "accident."

James's story begs the question: What would I do if I were in his shoes? In life, as much as it may feel that we weigh the facts and choose a direction based on the best conclusion the circumstances provide, our actions are dictated by the motivations of our personality. James was able to hack Rick's thumb off with an ax because he placed his friend's needs above his own. "I was so disgusted by the whole thing," he recalls. "I've never had a strong stomach. I can't even watch those emergency room shows on The Discovery Channel that my wife likes so much. So who knows where I got the nerve to go through with it? I just know I would've done anything to help Rick. That guy was like a brother to me." It's important to realize that James didn't really have much choice in the matter—though he was just a teenager at the time, he already possessed a keen ability to understand the needs of others coupled with a strong desire to put them before his own. When Rick approached him with this unusual request, James knew what he wanted to do—he'd rather put his friend through two months of pain than have him risk never feeling anything again. Putting other people first comes naturally to James; it's an enduring component of his character. Whether helping a friend move, taking his son to the park after school to practice throwing, or starting a mentoring program at his company, he comes alive in situations that call on him to help others. These are the places where he feels the satisfaction of following his heart. James was in his fifties before he realized that these lifelong tendencies are the product of his personality. Now he's armed with new knowledge that enables him to consciously use his personality to his advantage. Luckily, most of us won't have to wait this long to do the same.

The Baltimore Study

In the fall of 1958, volunteers started showing up at City Hospital in Baltimore. Prompted by a verbal chain letter that was snaking its way across the country, they came to see Dr. Nathan Shock, a wiry, balding researcher with an ambitious agenda that included following these people for the rest of their lives to monitor the physical and mental changes that surface during the normal course of aging. In a narrow hospital room cluttered with instruments, Dr. Shock and his team ran each participant through an intense three-day battery of more than one hundred physical and psychological tests. The research team asked each participant to return to Baltimore every other year, in order to repeat the identical series of tests. This testing regimen targeted a host of characteristics that were likely to change as the years passed. If enough people joined the study and stuck with it, trends would emerge in the data to illuminate the changes that anyone should expect to see in a lifetime.

Surprisingly, the participants just kept coming back to Baltimore. Even better, most brought a new recruit or two along on each return visit. Within four years of its inception, the aptly named Baltimore Longitudinal Study of Aging, or BLSA, had outgrown the 12,500 square feet of available space inside City Hospital. The study's ballooning potential caught the eye of Congress, which appropriated $7.5 million to build a permanent research facility on a five-acre plot donated by the city of Baltimore. One participant, Fred Litwin, joined the study in 1962 and—now in his seventies—still shows up for testing every twenty-four months. He also brings his wife, Evelyne, along. The Litwins are just a pair of the more than 2,500 people, ages twenty to ninety-seven, that the BLSA has tracked since 1958—though Fred holds the distinction of being the longest-running participant. When he speaks, the sparkle in his eyes reveals a zest that might otherwise lie hidden in the wrinkles of his skin: "If they can find out how the aging process works, I think that would be astonishing. I tend to dwell on the things that are behind the black curtain. . . . If they can be made less frightening, less distressing, and more predictable . . . I think that would be marvelous."

Fred owns a furniture store in downtown Washington, D.C., and the elevator in his building, installed during the 1850s, is the oldest working original elevator in the United States. Fred, like the elevator, is a pillar of longevity. In returning to Baltimore every couple years for the last four decades, he and the other participants of the BLSA have opened a fascinating window to the secrets of body and mind. The study has spawned more than a thousand publications detailing the physical and psychological changes that surface with age. We owe much of our understanding of things like diabetes, hardening of the arteries, obesity, Alzheimer's, intelligence, and personality directly to the observations made by the researchers in Baltimore. Whether changes occurred in the body, the mind, or the internal organs, the BLSA had markers ready to serve as witness. Some of these changes are encouraging—our vocabulary increases well into our eighties; while others—the body burns 120 fewer calories per day by age forty—point to the inevitable physical decline. Even a small change that's hardly noticeable in a single individual, such as the thickening of the heart wall that can happen to people with normal blood pressure, becomes a significant tool for determining better health care when it's observed in a large group of people.

It's ironic, but one of the most storied discoveries of the BLSA centers on a quality that didn't change at all with age—the personality. When Dr. Shock and his team designed the study in the 1950s, personality was well known as the essential ingredient behind why people do what they do. The researchers assumed, like the leading psychologists of the day, that personality traits were transient—vacillating in response to the changing circumstances life throws our way. They were certain to measure and track personality traits in the BLSA because they wanted to shed some light on which life events could trigger a shift in people's psychological makeup. If significant events like having children, reaching midlife, or retirement actually changed a person's personality, it was the

BLSA's mission to show people what to expect. Yet, twenty years into the study, there wasn't a scrap of data to support this assumption. Dr. Paul Costa, the head of the Laboratory of Personality and Cognition for the BLSA, explains, "Evidence says that after about age thirty personality becomes stabilized, age per se doesn't bring about any change. Personality has a huge influence over the life course, in terms of the choices that a person makes, careers, marriage, vocation, and interests." He continues, "People stay much the same in their basic dispositions, but these enduring traits lead them to particular and ever-changing lives." Recognizing that the tax dollars of the American public make the BLSA possible, Dr. Costa has spearheaded something of a crusade to make this knowledge public. It's a formidable undertaking, showing the world that everything it thinks it knows has been turned on its head. And if there is one thing that brain science has been trying to show us through the discoveries of the last decade, it's that our character is indeed our destiny.

Tragedy in the Ozarks

In 1984, Terry Wallis was a scrawny nineteen-year-old who loved to fix cars and crack jokes. Late one evening that July, he was driving a couple of friends down a mountain road when he lost control of his pickup, sending it vaulting over the guardrail and plunging more than twenty feet onto its roof in a dry riverbed below. One of his young companions perished, the other emerged unscathed, and Terry was left in a minimally conscious state with his body paralyzed from the neck down. Within months of the accident, his doctors had given up any hope of his recovery. Terry could breathe on his own, but he was unable to communicate, other than an occasional grunt or nod of the head. He stayed this way for the next nineteen years, trapped in a state his father, Jerry, describes as "there, but not there."

And then, on June 11, 2003, Terry brought his mother to her knees. She greeted him at the home that morning the same way she had every day for the last nineteen years, "Who's here? Who is it who came to visit you today?" But this time, Terry answered.

The walls seemed to come crashing in upon her as she watched her son's mouth release a brief, guttural reply. "Mom," he said. And then he asked her for a Pepsi.

By that afternoon, he was debating the merits of Pepsi versus Coke with his doctors, who were cautiously optimistic. They explained to the family that recoveries this late in the game were both incredibly rare and fraught with difficulty. The doctors shared cases like the police officer from Tennessee who emerged from an eight-year coma to a day of jokes and recounting annual winter camping trips, only to return to silence permanently eighteen hours later. But the more time passed, the more Terry proved he was above the odds. Words were replaced with phrases, and he even started moving his previously paralyzed limbs. He startled everyone by spontaneously remembering his Social Security number, and insisting that he was still nineteen years old. Terry had no memory of the years that had passed since the accident, but his life before the tragedy was still crystal clear. It took some convincing to get him to realize that nearly twenty years had gone by; he stubbornly tried to convince his father that Ronald Reagan was still the president. But Terry eventually acquiesced to the explanations offered by his family—it just took time for it to sink in that he was a human time capsule.

Neurologists estimate the chance of Terry's recovery at just 1 in 300 million, which raises the question of what made his recovery possible. Recognizing that they may never see another patient like Terry again, a team of researchers from the medical school at Cornell University—armed with the latest brain-imaging technology—took a look inside his head to find out. Using a new twist on the MRI called diffusion tensor imaging (DTI), they discovered the damage inside his brain was severe; it looked just like it did in patients who were still trapped in a semiconscious state. But they also noticed something highly unusual—cells in and around his cerebellum had branched out to grow new connections with the rest of his brain. The cerebellum is the brain's communication center. This fist-sized bundle of tissue comprises just 10% of the brain's total volume, yet it contains more neurons than the rest of the brain combined. The cerebellum ensures that the entire brain works in concert; when it loses contact with another part of the brain, it's as if that area ceases to exist. While Terry lay trapped in a semiconscious state, his cerebellum was busy growing new connections to replace those lost in the accident. It took nineteen years for these connections to reach a critical mass, but once they did Terry regained the ability to speak, to laugh, to love, and to go on living. His personality lay dormant for nearly two decades, and he emerged with the same motivations, preferences, and strengths as before the accident. He's still quick to crack a joke, slow to change his opinion, and interested in what kind of car you drive—as long as it isn't a Chevy.

Terry Wallis recovered consciousness because our brains are plastic. At first glance, this may not seem like the most flattering term for the most complicated organ in the body, but it's an excellent way to remember how neuroplasticity works. Like plastic, the regions of the brain are apt to maintain a persistent structure and function, but they can make important

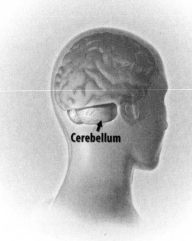

Cerebellum

Terry Wallis awoke from nineteen years in a semiconscious state thanks to significant new cell growth in the cerebellum. Long underestimated due to its location underneath the brain, this fist-sized structure, researchers have discovered, plays the essential role of processing center for the vast amounts of information traveling throughout the brain.

adjustments under the right kind of pressure. Each of the brain's 100 billion cells communicates by branching off small branches to reach out to other cells. A single cell can grow 15,000 connections with its neighbors, and these connections are sprouted and pruned as they are needed. When enough cells build connections in concert, they pave entirely new pathways for information to travel in the brain. Researchers studying brain plasticity have learned that some areas are more prone to growth than others. In fact, some areas of the brain are so opposed to organized change that they're considered "frozen"—unable to build pathways that will affect their function substantially.

When the Baltimore Longitudinal Study of Aging began in 1958, researchers could only map the brain according to the different functions performed by its four main divisions, known as lobes. These days, we can pinpoint the purpose of different brain regions with far greater specificity. For example, personality is predominantly housed in the right orbitofrontal cortex (ROC), directly above the right eye. We tend not to see changes in personality in adulthood because the ROC has lost its plasticity by this point. Personality forms like molding clay. When we're born, our personality lacks form; it takes its shape as we move toward adulthood. And reaching adulthood is the neural equivalent of throwing your project in the kiln—the shape it's in is the shape in which it's going to stay. This process isn't dictated solely by our environment, because genes have an important influence on the molding. Just as clays have texture—some are suited for hand-built objects, while others are ideal for throwing—we have genetic predispositions that determine how our personality is formed.

Throughout childhood and adolescence the ROC is highly plastic. By the time we reach adulthood, the plasticity of the ROC is lost and our personality is imprinted in the brain. The ROC gradually takes over more and more of our thinking as it becomes hardwired. Some inclinations are reinforced and stabilized during this development, while others become increasingly difficult to access. The cerebellum may be the brain's communication center, but the ROC provides command and control—the rest of the brain becomes dependent upon the master plan that's written there. To illustrate how this process works, I need to put you in a little contest. Your opponent is a young child, just nine years old. You'll be in separate rooms for the event, where you'll each take a seat in front of a monitor. On the table in front of the screen is a large red button. On your screens you'll each see an identical series of about fifty circles, presented one at a time. Each circle will have a striped or solid pattern. If the circle that flashes on your screen is solid, I want you to hit

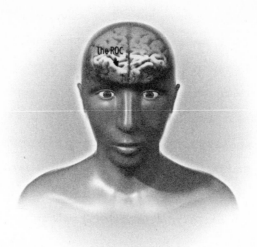

Recent advances in neuroscience pinpoint the physical location of personality in the brain–the right orbitofrontal cortex (ROC). Located directly above the right eye, the cells in the ROC take shape throughout childhood and adolescence. By the time we reach adulthood this malleability is lost and our personality is permanently imprinted in the brain. The ROC contains the master plan for our behavior that controls the vast majority of what we do and say each day.

your button once, as quickly as you can. If the circle is striped, you do nothing. I'll be measuring your reaction time on the solid circles to see who can hit the button the fastest. Sound easy enough? Okay, then I'll switch things around on you. I'm going to show you another set of circles, but this time you should smack your button when the circle is striped, not when it's solid. A little harder, yes? Think you'll still be able to react faster than a child? Researchers at the Shriver Center in Massachusetts, one of the leading child brain research centers in the world, would bet against you. The game I've just described is part of a study they're conducting on brain plasticity in the area around the ROC. When the rules switch, and the task requires clicking on the opposite circle, children are much faster than adults. Their reaction time is actually quite similar between the two trials, whereas adult reaction time slows when we're required to change. What's behind this? The researchers at the Shriver Center scan participants' brains while they complete both tasks, and they've found—for adults only—that the second trial activates the area around the ROC, where years of patterned behavior is stored. This is what slows the adults down. Children complete the second task at the same speed as the first because this area in their brain is less developed— there isn't enough happening there to slow down their reaction time.

Cracking the Code

The first documented witness to personality was a physician on a small island in the southeastern corner of Greece. In 440 B.C. this freethinking doctor by the name of Hippocrates abandoned the superstitious practices of his contemporaries and conducted detailed observations of his patients prior to reaching a diagnosis. This may not sound very innovative by today's standards, but in a world that relied on mythology to understand illness, Hippocrates' practices were a 180-degree turn from the norm. As he assiduously observed his patients' symptoms and behavior, he was struck by the profound influence of the mind on the body and came to the conclusion that, "It's far more important to know what person the disease has than what disease the person has." Hippocrates was eager to understand the source of his patients' behavior, and he came to identify four distinct traits that surfaced in varying degrees in all people. He called these traits "humors," and—even though he couldn't fathom how they were controlled by the brain—he was the first to recognize what we now know as personality. Hippocrates' theories dominated the field of medicine for nearly two thousand years.

By the time William Marston was born in 1893, the world's grasp of personality had yet to evolve. Marston grew up in a small town in rural Massachusetts that was a buggy ride away from a powerful new movement happening in Cambridge. A Harvard professor, William James, would acquaint a legion of readers during the late 1800s and early 1900s with the new science of psychology. James's immensely popular and aptly named book *The Principles of Psychology* made an assertion that left a lasting impression on Marston, during his own studies at Harvard: "It is well for the world that in most of us, by the age of thirty, the character has set like plaster, and will never soften again." To Marston, this suggestion harked back to the notion of permanent dispositions of character witnessed by Hippocrates. By the time Marston received his Ph.D. in psychology from Harvard in 1921, he was well down the path of discovering the essence of personality.

Marston's broad shoulders, prominent chin, and piercing, deeply set eyes gave him an intimidating appearance that could hide his curious and affable demeanor. But Marston was no intellectual pussycat—he had an uncanny ability to find solutions to tough problems in connections between seemingly disparate concepts. True to form, his quest to find the truth about personality began with studying liars and his creativity led to the invention of the polygraph, or lie detector test. Marston noticed that telling a lie is a surefire way to get the body to feel emotion. This emotion can be worry, shame, excitement, or most anything, really—it all depends upon why the lie is being told. When we speak the truth, it doesn't send the body on a similar emotional roller coaster. Good liars fool us into thinking they're telling the truth by hiding these emotions from our view. Regardless of what they are feeling, they look us in the eye, speak smoothly, and project confidence—just like someone who is speaking the truth. But inside the body of anyone telling a lie—whether it's a little white one or a real whopper—there are physiological responses that accompany the feelings. These responses include changes in blood pressure, breathing, and the skin's ability to conduct electricity, and they're present whether the liar is conscious of them or not. It was Marston's invention of a simple machine—the polygraph—that showed the subtle physiological changes that inevitably surface when someone is lying. A polygraph can expose the savviest of liars, no matter how skilled they are at getting others to think they speak the truth.

When Marston studied liars, he was actually studying all of us. Lying is a social norm we use to save people's feelings, avoid conflict, or achieve gains. Even if we don't like to admit it, most people lie on a regular basis. Truth be told, a little more than half of us admit that it's all right to lie in certain situations. Yet when researchers track people, they find that 97% of us don't tell a lie just every once in a while—we tell an average of one whopper per day! Every time one of Marston's subjects told a lie, he stopped to ask questions. He found that different people lied for different reasons, but the same individual would usually lie for the same reason. And this is where Marston saw the connection—people told lies when a situation was very important to them. For most people, telling lies wasn't a big part of their behavioral repertoire, but the reason for the lie was. Some were motivated to lie to help out a friend, others to smooth a difficult conversation, others to keep themselves in control, and so on. People's motivation for lying revealed something important about their own needs. When Marston followed this clue further he noticed the same needs controlled much of what someone would say and do each day—they revealed the predictable tendencies of human personality.

The DISC Model

Like Hippocrates before him, Marston saw personality existing along four unique dimensions, or traits. Though these personality traits represent needs that are important to everyone to some degree, knowing which is predominant in any person is the key to understanding personality. Marston's four personality traits are referred to as the DISC model, which is an acronym for a person's tendency to be Dominant, Interpersonal, Steady, or Conscientious.

People high in the "Dominant" trait are direct and assertive. They think independently, are ambitious, and take a quick and active approach to solving problems. Dominants are competitive and enjoy a challenge even when the odds are stacked against them. They have a strong need to achieve and try to maintain a measure of authority and control over the environment in which they live and work. Other people find them determined and strong willed, which is no surprise, as Dominants like to have things done their way.

People high in the "Interpersonal" trait are entertaining and social. They like to participate in groups and rely on their social skills as the primary means for getting things done. Highly extroverted, these people are considered by others to be friendly and outgoing. They have a consistent urge to meet and talk with other people, and they may even try to bring people who are less sociable together. Interpersonal people are often considered to be emotional because they readily express their feelings and are generally more comfortable with emotions than others.

People high in the "Steady" trait are persistent and patient. They take a measured, stable approach to life and don't like surprises. They are accommodating and undemanding, often showing intense loyalty to those around them. Steady people place a high value on sincerity; they habitually tell the truth and expect others to do the same. People tend to see them as deliberate and consistent in their approach to life, which can lead to the label of being predictable. Steady individuals possess an unusual level of persistence, and can maintain their focus and interest in something longer than most others can.

People high in the "Conscientious" trait are interested in precision and accuracy. They like structure and details, and they focus intensely on the facts. They regard tradition and etiquette as highly important and will extend great effort to support such mores. Conscientious individuals tend to use a systematic approach to their activities, and will insist on the use of rules in order to manage or control their environments. They are understated and indirect in approaching conflict and may postpone taking action until it is absolutely necessary. This can lead others to see them as passive and compliant.

Marston's DISC model captures what people tend to think, feel, and do as a product of the inherent tendencies of their personality. There are certainly more layers of depth to the DISC model—and we will explore them in later chapters—but the image of the DISC model of personality provides a quick visual to illustrate the global differences between the four DISC personality traits. Along the vertical axes, the traits are distinguished by the general tendency to be *active* or *reactive* to things. That is, do I tend to act quickly when things change, or am I more likely to sit back and see how things play out first? Along the horizontal axes the

The modernized version of the DISC model of personality—first introduced by Harvard psychologist William Marston in 1928. The DISC model examines the motivations for people's behavior along four unique dimensions or traits. Though these personality traits represent needs that are important for everyone to some degree, knowing which tendency is predominant in any person is the key to understanding personality.

traits are distinguished by the general tendency to focus more on *tasks* or *people*. We all lean unconsciously toward one or the other.

DISC personality profiling first gained prominence during the massive buildup of the U.S. military during the Second World War. Assessing the DISC profiles of new recruits provided an objective method for matching them to the right assignment. The military lacked a DISC test and relied upon hours of interviews and interpretation by psychologists for each recruit. Still, the DISC profiles eliminated a significant amount of trial and error in getting a new soldier to the right placement. After the war, many of these soldiers brought the DISC model with them into civilian life. They were instrumental in spreading the word that produced a silent movement dedicated to the continued study, use, and refinement of the DISC model long after Marston's death in 1947. For several decades this movement has endured, thanks to a cadre of academics and trainers who recognize the value of DISC profiling and have the training necessary to use it. So far, they've helped 50 million people to discover the source of their strengths, and DISC remains the most widely used personality model in the world today.

Decades of DISC research have led to three major improvements in DISC since Marston's death. First, the terms in Marston's model have been updated to keep the language current. The second improvement is rooted in the discovery that each of us is more than just a D, I, S, or C. Since everyone displays each of these traits to some degree, the trait that prevails doesn't tell the whole story. A complete look at a personality profile comes in understanding how we blend these four traits. If you want to understand someone, it's still important to know which DISC trait dominates, but the discovery of the fourteen unique personality types makes it even easier to know where people are coming from. These types are more than one-word labels; they identify the most recognizable and useful differences among people. The fourteen types provide a common language and understanding of how each of us responds to others, prefers to complete tasks, and manages time and energy (all found in Chapter 4). The third DISC innovation ensures that you can learn your type and personality profile. In the early years, understanding your DISC profile required hours of interviews and interpretation by psychologists. With the advent of the Internet and improvements in psychological assessment, it's now possible to test yourself online to discover your personality profile quickly and accurately. Instructions for accessing your online administration of this newest version, the IDISC personality profiler, are in Chapter 3. While you can still learn a lot from this book without testing yourself, knowing your precise profile makes the learning real and serves as the foundation for how you understand personality.

2: Self-Awareness Breeds Success

P*RESS YOUR LUCK* was the immensely popular 1980s game show that featured the illustrious Big Board—a massive, slot-machine-like wall of cash and prizes. Contestants had the simple, albeit nerve-wracking job of pressing a red plunger-shaped button that froze the board in place. Each smack of the button landed on cash, vacations, valuable prizes, or the dreaded Whammy—a detestable little animated monster that would roller-skate, ski, even moonwalk his way across the screen to snatch up cash and prizes. The game was called *Press Your Luck,* because the inevitable threat of the bankrupting Whammy ensured that each trip to the Big Board was a major risk. When a player was satisfied with her winnings, she could pass her remaining "spins" on to another contestant and sidestep any further risk of losing it all to the Whammy.

From the show's debut in September 1983, Michael Larson was its biggest fan. The unemployed ice cream truck driver from Ohio never missed an episode. One day, he noticed something strange about the Big Board—it felt like he could predict when a Whammy was going to come up. To test his theory, he recorded every episode of the show for six straight weeks and followed the Big Board frame by frame on a series of televisions he set up in his living room. He discovered the Big Board didn't really follow a randomized path, but rather one of six predictable sequences. Michael perfected his technique on each day's episode, training himself to stop the board when he was certain it wouldn't land on a Whammy. Finally convincing his girlfriend that he was going to be rich, he emptied their bank account and bought a one-way ticket to Los Angeles to try out for the show.

At the audition, Michael was quick to catch the attention of the show's producers. "He really impressed us," executive producer Bill Carruthers remembers. "He had charisma, he played the game very well. Here was this out-of-work ice cream guy who told us he loved the show so much he flew out on his own to try to get on." Bob Edwards, the contestant coordinator, wasn't so sure. "There was something about the guy that worried me." Edwards felt like there was something a little "off" about this man from Ohio. With his chubby cheeks, salt-and-pepper beard, and persistent grin, he seemed more like a shopping mall Santa Claus than a game show contestant. The producers debated at length before deciding to let him on the show. On May 19, 1984, Michael went to the studio and finally had his shot at getting rich.

The first half of the episode was relatively uneventful. Michael's nervous first spin landed on a Whammy, and he earned just $2,500 with his remaining spins. The final round, however, was something entirely different. He started the round with seven spins, but needed just one to do his bidding. Michael went first and methodically alternated between one of seven spaces that awarded him $750 to $5,000 in cash, plus another spin. The tension started to grow when Michael accumulated

$30,000 in his bank. It was more money than anyone had ever earned on the program, yet Michael continued to press his luck. With each successful smack of the button, he increased his already bulging bankroll and whipped the audience further into frenzy. He continued past the $40,000, $50,000, and even $60,000 marks. The show's affable host, Peter Tomarken, begged him to stop, fearing he would lose it all to a Whammy. Michael pressed on.

As he approached the $100,000 mark, things started to get tricky. The half-hour program had never run over, yet Michael's spinning had already sent it well past the hour mark. Adding insult to injury, Whammies provided natural breaks in the action that CBS relied upon to air commercials. It was pretty clear by this point that Michael wasn't going to be hitting any Whammies. Michael Brockman, CBS's head of daytime programming, was relaxing at home when he received a call from the *Press Your Luck* production assistants. "Something was very wrong," he recalls. "Here was this guy from nowhere, and he was hitting the bonus box every time. It was bedlam, I can tell you. And we couldn't stop this guy. He was going to own CBS in a few minutes. He kept going around the board and hitting that box." After a flurry of phone calls they decided against pulling the plug on Michael. Spotting the panic among the production team, Michael burned through his remaining spins in short order and walked with $110,237 in cash and prizes. Since he hadn't done anything illegal, CBS let him keep his winnings. They aired his episodes just once (at more than double the ratings of a typical episode), immediately added additional sequences to the game board, and eventually installed the technology required to produce a truly randomized sequence of squares. When they sold the show to the USA Network for syndication, Michael Larson's episodes weren't part of the package.

Michael's life after the show reveals just how much he lacked self-awareness, and how utterly destructive a personality can be when it rips along unabated. He took his winnings and continued to press his luck. The first major Whammy came on the wrong end of a real estate Ponzi scheme in Ohio. He continued looking furiously for another code to crack, when a local radio station offered $30,000 to anyone who could produce two dollar bills with consecutive serial numbers. He went to the bank and took out the $50,000 remaining from his winnings—in one-dollar bills. Day after day, Larson and his girlfriend sorted the money in piles that spread throughout their home. And they never finished. While out at a Christmas party one evening, their home was broken into and the money stolen. Once again broke and unemployed, Larson called the producers of *Press Your Luck* with a defiant request: "I know you've added patterns to the board, but I bet I can beat you again. How about a tournament of champions?" CBS passed, and Michael Larson never had another win.

Multiple Minds

Michael Larson's life provides a glimpse of the fleeting highs and inevitable lows that surface when one leans blindly on his personality. When our natural tendencies go unchecked, our unique abilities only serve us to a point, and our weaknesses bring us down abruptly. The ingenuity Michael displayed in cracking the Big Board was a very successful, albeit highly unusual, effort. He was undeterred by the complexity of the Board—even enticed by it—because his personality made him a creative problem solver. Motivated by his desire to beat the Big Board, he spent weeks methodically dissecting the patterns frame by frame in his living room. But—like many others who are energized by creativity— Michael's weakness was impulsivity. He continued along capriciously, searching for another puzzle to crack. He never even considered putting the kibosh on his elaborate scheming, and was even surprised when he lost everything. As renowned neurologist Antonio Damasio puts it, "Nature is not that inventive when it comes to successful solutions. Once it works, it tries it again and again."

No strength can always serve us without direction, and self-awareness is the single, critical skill that enables us to understand and even manage our ingrained personality. Self-awareness is a flexible skill that increases with effort and decreases without it, and, for most of us, the latter applies. In the TalentSmart study, it was startling to discover that only 29% of the people we tested possessed a solid understanding of their own tendencies. It seems the vast majority of us are largely uncertain as to how we come across to others, and we're not yet skilled at tracking our strengths to ensure that they're put to good use. More than 70% of those we tested had considerable difficulty managing the stress and interpersonal conflict that are fostered by this lack of self-awareness.

We also compared people's levels of self-awareness to their ability to achieve the things they found most important in life. We found that as self-awareness increases, people's satisfaction with life skyrockets, and they are far more likely to reach their goals at work and at home. These people take the time to first learn, and then understand, their style for responding to challenges and opportunities. They recognize the situations and people that will make them successful, and this makes it easy to follow the right path. They understand the limiting tendencies they can't avoid, and this helps them to spot when this is happening and minimize the damage that results. Finally, they know what they really want out of life, and this understanding paves the way to getting it. Self-awareness is such a pervasive tendency in success that it transcends age, intelligence, education, profession, and job level. Across virtually every profession and industry, we found that 83% of top performers are high in self-awareness, whereas just 2% of low performers possess this critical skill. Those who understand their preferences and tendencies are far more likely to pursue the right opportunities, put their strengths to work, and get the results they desire.

The top performers in the TalentSmart study show us that self-awareness is more a journey than a destination. Stewart Coleman is a

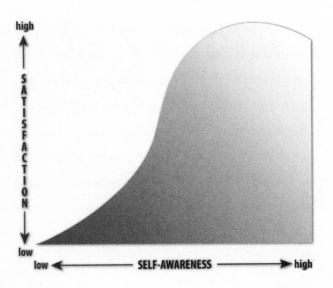

As we studied successful people, a clear trend emerged revealing a critical thing they have in common: an acute sense of self-awareness. As people's self-awareness increases, they better understand the prevailing tendencies of their personality that hold sway over so much of what they do and say each day. Those with higher levels of self-awareness have a far greater tendency to capitalize on their strengths, minimize the effects of their weaknesses, and put themselves in the position to succeed.

man whose life personifies this process. When I sat down with him, the fifty-eight-year-old software executive talked so comfortably about his tendencies that self-awareness appeared to come naturally, like a God-given element of his persona. But this wasn't always the case. As a boy, Stewart had an inquisitive mind—he created most of his own toys by combining discarded household items. As the youngest of five children, he was the "runt of the litter" and was picked on often. He learned to mind his business by avoiding anything that would bring him attention. He carried this attitude into high school, a time when many of his peers seemed to crave the spotlight. By the time he was a sophomore, he learned that the only way to avoid being bullied by the older classmen (and classwomen) was to befriend them. It took a lot of energy to break free from the caste that made him who he was—the introverted shy-guy.

In college, Stewart expended a tremendous amount of energy to compensate for his shyness. He made friendships that ultimately proved the effort he expended in cultivating relationships was a wise choice. "When I graduated from college with an engineering degree, there weren't a lot of good jobs in Phoenix for people with my background," he remembers, "so a friend helped me get a job at his father's restaurant." Stewart's attention to detail and drive to succeed served him well in the restaurant business. He was proud of the accomplishment, but came home each night exhausted and overwhelmed from having to constantly deal with people—so many conflicts and unique needs. "I was offered a regional management position with another restaurant, but passed on that and moved to Santa Clara. I thought working as an engineer would solve all my people problems." But it didn't. His initiative and work ethic sent him climbing up the corporate ladder, yet more and more, his professional success and happiness were based on his ability to inspire and motivate others. To succeed in this, he found himself returning to the same focus on relationships he had "created" in high school and college.

"I wasn't content working on a single [software] application," Stewart explains, "I wanted to develop systems that would catapult the entire company forward." And he learned very quickly that this had to be accomplished through people. The trick for Stewart—which he regards as the secret to his success—was understanding that he couldn't approach "the people stuff" as naturally as some of his coworkers. His tendency toward introversion continues—he's still driven, headstrong, and exhausted by social interaction. Hours of working alone at his desk don't leave him feeling worn out, like he does if working in a group. But Stewart succeeds because he knows this about himself, and manages his schedule accordingly. "I treat people like a project," he says. "Some aspects of my job are more taxing than others, and the social stuff is a part of that. I just budget my time, and give people my full attention when it's their time." Stewart is able and willing to reach out to people; he just has to do it consciously.

Stewart's journey to self-awareness has come from years of self-reflection, not a New Year's resolution or short-lived motivational stint. He understands his unchanging personality well, because he's taken the time to get intimately familiar with his tendencies, strengths, and shortcomings. The looming challenge with self-awareness is that most of us grossly overestimate the accuracy with which we perceive our own behavior. But it's really understanding the whole picture that serves us. The more we consider the beauty and the blemishes, the more we can put them both to work to achieve what we want. Stewart knows he has even more to learn about himself if he wants to take his game to the next level. His professional ambition has not subsided as a senior executive; he wants to lead his company to number one in the industry. Our meeting runs twenty minutes over time before Stewart steps out of his reflection and explains that he has work to return to before an afternoon meeting. We shake hands and the phone rings as I make my way to the door. The inflection in Stewart's voice goes up a notch as he responds to an update on the other end of the phone, "Thanks for keeping me up to speed on this situation, Joyce. And I hope your bulldog is feeling better."

Personality is a powerful factor in life that dictates much of what we find comfortable and motivating. Yet, as Stewart Coleman reveals, personality doesn't have to control everything we do—we can use self-awareness to retain a choice in the matter. The area of the brain responsible for self-awareness is highly malleable. But like a muscle, just having it doesn't mean it will be put to good use. Our self-awareness needs to be exercised before it can get strong. Discovering your personality profile can accelerate this process. Since your profile captures the essence of your strengths, weaknesses, and general tendencies, identifying your type eliminates much of the struggle on the road to self-awareness.

Personality is the single pervasive artifact of the mind that determines human behavior. Since your profile doesn't change, aligning your efforts with it is the only way you can use it to your advantage. In the next chapter, you'll begin the journey to increased self-awareness in earnest. By completing the IDISC personality profiler, you'll discover which of the fourteen profiles you are, as well as the degree to which you possess each of the four DISC traits. Study your IDISC results carefully. They'll help you to do two important things. You'll develop an intimate familiarity with your strengths, and gain an understanding of your weaknesses that ensures you can tackle problems while they are big enough to see, yet still small enough to solve. This process is critical because success doesn't come from changing ourselves into someone we are not. It comes from knowing who we are.

3: The IDISC Personality Profiler

THE EIGHT-DIGIT access code for the IDISC personality profiler printed on the inside of the dust jacket of this book is a unique number specifically for your use. Type the following address into your Web browser: www.personalitycode.com. Click the navigation at the top of the page that says "Take the test," and follow the instructions on the page. When the system asks for your ID code, you will need to type in the code from the inside of your book jacket. You can type the letters in capital or lowercase form; it does not matter. The only technical requirements are a computer with Internet access, a Web browser, and a 56K modem or faster.

Code Inside Book Jacket

8XG44K32

TUMY76UE

Your passcode to take the online IDISC personality profiler is located on the backside of the dust jacket of this book. Just remove the dust jacket, and you'll see the eight-digit access code printed on the lower right-hand side. This code is a unique number specifically for you, and will give you access to the test at www.personalitycode.com.

Very few people find the test difficult or stressful to complete. Since the IDISC asks straightforward questions about your behavior, you already have all of the answers. When you complete the test, it will instantly create your score profile. You will see your results immediately and can return to view them anytime. The system will also let you print your results and save them as a document on your computer. How much time you spend reviewing your score profile and participating in the online activities is really up to you. Some people spend just ten or twenty minutes reading through their results. Others, over the course of a few months, will use all of the ten hours of activities available.

The questions take just fifteen minutes to complete. Just click "Done" and the magic happens—a hundred thousand lines of programmed code can run in under a second. Forget waiting for someone to hand score a dense booklet; your results are in front of you faster than getting a stock quote. Most people who take the test don't consider the questions too prying, yet behind-the-scenes statistical analyses examine the pattern of responses to crack the personality code. Regardless, the information you enter in taking the test is stored on a secure, remote server that is monitored twenty-four hours a day to ensure that no one will have access to your results.

The Purpose of the Test

Recent advancements in psychological science have confirmed that the vast majority of our behavior is determined by our personality—stable traits of individual character that remain unchanged throughout a lifetime. Yet these discoveries have languished in academic obscurity to the point that most of us have very little understanding of how our personality actually determines our fate. Understanding our principal tendencies, motivations, and preferences is a formidable challenge because the brain is the most complex organ in the body. Just compare it to another critical organ, the heart. If you want to understand the state your heart is in, you can visit a cardiologist who, after a couple of tests, will be able to tell you everything you need to know. Bring your heart to him, and he can examine it, look inside it, and scan it until virtually no mystery remains as to how it functions. Why can't we do the same thing with our brains? The billion or so neurons in the brain make this three-pound lump of tissue a hard one to size up. This densely tangled web simultaneously controls the senses, movement, behavior, memory, learning, heart rate, blood pressure, fluid balance, and body temperature. But just as your heart's pumping is seen in the circulation of blood throughout your body, your brain's functioning is seen in behavior: what you do and say on a daily basis.

Patterns in behavior provide the greatest clues to how a person thinks and what they'll do next. The only problem is that these patterns can be hard to understand if you don't know what you're looking for. Each of us has powerful experiences in life that are windows of varying sizes to our personality. They shed light on our tendencies and preferences, but we lack the larger perspective needed to integrate them into a cohesive whole. So, how can we each discover the "code" to our personality? One way would be to monitor and record your behavior over a prolonged period of time to capture the tendencies and preferences that indicate your type. Of course this would be a difficult endeavor, and likely a fruitless one, as our perception of our actions tends to be inaccurate. We could have another person do the tracking for us, but who could provide the level of 24/7 understanding needed to accurately rate us? Objectivity comes in a test. In our search to crack the personality code, we developed the world's most popular profiling system into an easy-to-use online personality profiler, the IDISC. The IDISC is significant because it allows you to go online and discover an objective and scientifically valid measure of your personality profile in minutes. The unique access number included in this book is all you need to open the test questions online and, with the click of your mouse, have your profile instantly analyzed. The test reveals how much you rely on the four DISC dimensions of behavior, and it analyzes this combination to provide your personality type.

Measuring your personality moves this book beyond a factual exercise. Knowing your profile makes the learning real, relevant, and personal. The value of testing yourself is akin to learning the waltz with an actual partner. If I tell you how the dance works you are likely to learn something and may even get the urge to try it yourself. If you practice each step with a partner as I show you the waltz, your chances for remembering the steps later on the dance floor go up exponentially. The personality profile you receive from the IDISC will be your dance partner as you move through the strategies presented in the remainder of this book. It will remind you where to step with every beat of the music. As you read the remaining chapters and learn how to put your personality to use, it's essential to know your own profile. It will help you to reflect upon where you stand, and where in your life you can apply new knowledge the most. No test can do this for you, but your IDISC profile will help you to understand your tendencies, preferences, and motivations. If you choose to take the IDISC personality profiler, you will expand your self-awareness by discovering the source of your strengths and learning how to sidestep your weaknesses. We learned in the

TalentSmart study that this act is critical to success. People who increase their self-awareness through the careful consideration of their personality profile are far more likely to reach their goals at work and at home.

Inside the IDISC

The recent profusion of "personality" tests has contributed to a false understanding of how personality shapes our lives. Why is this? These tests are little more than a way of classifying and labeling obvious differences among people. The arbitrary distinctions offered by these tests are either experimentally untested, or they've failed to hold up when held to the light of experimental scrutiny. While these tests can be fun, they create a false sense of security. We tend to gravitate toward anything labeled a "personality" test because it's a fundamental component of who we are. It's tough because most people don't know how to evaluate the validity of the test they are taking, and they end up receiving feedback that is essentially irrelevant. The spate of tests giving a false understanding of personality has become more than an academic issue. These days, you don't have to be a reader of the *Journal of Abnormal Psychology* to find articles on the perils of personality testing—it's a growing public concern that's popping up in major media outlets like *Time* magazine and *The New York Times*. Annie Murphy Paul, who explores the matter in depth in her book *The Cult of Personality*, explains, "Despite their prevalence—and the importance of the matters they are called upon to decide—personality tests have received surprisingly little scrutiny. Personality testing has thrived in the shade of casual neglect, growing unchecked along with abuses like invasive questions, inaccurate labels, and unjust outcomes."

We're misguided by the inability of these tests to tap the real power of personality in our lives. Despite the clear experiential testimony, most of us remain sadly in the dark about the essential code of human behavior, knowing more about the astrological traits of ourselves and others than we do about our own personalities. The IDISC personality profiler is a modernized method for measuring the traits first introduced by William Marston, whose personality profiling system is the longest-standing and most widely utilized model in the world. The DISC model has withstood more than seventy years of scrutiny, evaluation, and modification because it's both scientifically sound and highly intuitive. Since you can decipher but can't change your "code," the real power of personality lies in making your strengths and tendencies work for you. But prior to the IDISC, learning your DISC profile was a painstaking process. The IDISC simplifies this process with analyses of your instinctive reactions and response pattern against 123,000 possible configurations. Your results instantly reveal which of the fourteen personality types best describes you, as well as a detailed analysis of your tendency to use the four DISC behavioral traits: Dominant, Interpersonal, Steady, and Conscientious. (For common questions about the IDISC, see Appendix A.)

When you test as many people as we did during the course of the TalentSmart study, you learn quickly that subjects tend to take their results very seriously. When people take a test that measures the degree to which they possess some quality—emotional intelligence is a good example—it can be a threatening experience. Even a skeptical executive who just heard the term for the first time that morning doesn't want to be told he has a low score. This concern is well founded, yet it is unrelated to the IDISC. None of the personality traits measured by the IDISC is better than any other. We all possess these traits in varying degrees. With the vast majority of our behavior controlled by our personality, understanding the strengths and weaknesses of your profile is essential. Those who understand their personality first bring themselves more quickly and accurately into focus.

The IDISC presents a series of 112 adjectives that are paired into twenty-eight groups of four. As you move through each quartet of words, you are forced to choose one from the set that most describes you and another from the set that least describes you. This process takes about fifteen minutes to complete, and your results are permanently stored online. You can return to your results to review them whenever you wish. Inside your results profile is an e-learning program that helps to bring the DISC traits to life—and the fourteen personality types into which they merge—with clips from movies, television, and real-world events that illustrate personality in action. An automated goal-tracking system summarizes the steps you're taking to improve your self-awareness and provides automatic reminders via e-mail to help you stay on track. What you'll learn about your personality profile is relevant for use at work and at home, as this stable facet of your character is engaged in every aspect of your life. You'll discover the unique strengths of your profile, as well as the tendencies that bring you down when they go unchecked. And the objectivity provided by the online test ensures that you'll learn far more about your personality than you ever could on your own.

4: The Fourteen Types of People

SHAQUILLE O'NEAL STANDS more than seven feet tall, weighs 350 pounds, and wears a size 22 shoe. Considered one of the fifty greatest NBA players of all time, the opinionated and outspoken veteran tends to think pretty highly of himself. Of the five nicknames he's given himself in his fifteen-year career, Superman is his favorite—he has the logo tattooed on his arm, painted on his car, and stitched into his sheets. Shaq isn't the guy you want in your face when you make a bad call, but Bob Delaney doesn't seem to mind. "I don't feel any level of intimidation," he says. "I don't feel any level of not being able to handle the situation."

The veteran referee has always been calm under pressure, a quality that has put him in two of the more vicelike jobs on the planet. Prior to his career in the NBA, Delaney went undercover to infiltrate the mob. The year was 1973 and Delaney was a twenty-three-year-old New Jersey state trooper. His superiors invited him to join Project Alpha, a joint initiative with the FBI that sought to take down the DiNorsico crime family. Delaney jumped at the chance. Using the pseudonym Bobby Covert, he spent more than two years living the life of a mobster. It was slow going at first—the mob doesn't just open the door for anybody—but the FBI found Bobby a way in through a family consigliere turned informant. Their agreement was simple—the informant received immunity and Bobby was treated like a friend. If either lost his cover, they were both dead.

Before long, Bobby was raking in six-figure hauls for the mob. He ran a business, Alamo Transportation, as a front for transporting stolen goods. But he couldn't stop there, not if he wanted to survive. "You can't just make believe," Delaney says. "You've got to become that person. Me being president of Alamo Transportation . . . there were mornings when I was concerned more about the trucks and the profit level than anything else." He made emergency trips across the country for mob bosses, and was soon involved in extortion and loan-sharking. On the outside, Bobby Covert kept his cool. He regularly wore wires to meetings where members of the mob would heap incriminating evidence upon their operation. "I would dress like them, I would act like them as much as I could," he recalls. "I would be very good at being able to have a conversation." Even though he was never suspected as a snitch, on the inside Bob Delaney was sweating bullets. It took everything he had to keep himself together. "I was doing the kiss on the cheeks, the whole thing, and I would leave a meeting and pull over to the side of the road to throw up. Or I would stop at the first gas station because I had diarrhea. No one knew about that. No one could know. Informants die in that world."

When the bust finally happened, Bob Delaney's undercover work sent twenty-nine mobsters to jail. Delaney was so good at convincing them that he was one of them that the mobsters refused to believe he was a cop. At the bust, Bob stood with the FBI while the mobsters were paraded in front of them in handcuffs. One of his associates yelled over to him from the line, "Hey, Bobby! What'd they pinch ya for?" It was a surreal moment. As are many in the NBA. Today Bob Delaney is one of the most respected referees in professional basketball, due in large part to his uncanny ability to keep a level head. This isn't an easy thing to do when you're standing on the floor of an arena that's swelling with 40,000 screaming fans—all of whom agree with that seven-foot Goliath who's in your face over a bad call. That's the life of an NBA referee. It's a tough job, but one for which Bob Delaney's personality is perfectly suited.

Discovering the Fourteen Types

Bob Delaney discovered the strengths of his personality—such as his ability to remain "smooth under pressure"—through years of gut-wrenching trial and error. Thankfully you won't have to undergo similar trials to harness the power in your personality type. By now you should have gone online to take the IDISC and learned which of the fourteen personality types best describes you (instructions for accessing the test are in Chapter 3). As you read the detailed descriptions of the fourteen types in this chapter, remember that each represents a unique combination of the four core DISC behavioral traits: Dominant, Interpersonal, Steady, and Conscientious. Whether your type is that of the Detective, Diplomat, Coach, or any of the fourteen, the name is not meant to indicate your profession. Rather, it's a single descriptive term that captures the essence of the unique strengths and challenges of your personality type.

The fourteen personality types represent the most recognizable and useful differences among people. When you discover someone's type, it makes it easy to understand where they are coming from—it reveals how they react to their environment, how they prefer to complete tasks, and what they do to manage their time and energy. For each type, you'll learn the defining characteristics of those that hold it. You'll find out how often it's seen in the public at large, as well as famous figures who shared this type and capitalized on it. Study the ins and outs of the descriptions of those closest to you, and you'll begin to see them in a whole new light.

The Fourteen Personality Types

(and the percentage of the population sharing each type)

Ally	5%
Architect	13%
Coach	9%
Detective	9%
Diplomat	9%
Entrepreneur	7%
Expert	6%
Innovator	3%
Mobilizer	3%
Motivator	13%
Opportunist	2%
Researcher	4%
Sponsor	16%
Strategist	1%

The **Ally**

You value the quality of your relationships over most other things. You have a keen ability to connect with other people, which is a highly visible element of this profile that is only seen in 5% of the population. Your people skills come in handy during conflict, because you  can maneuver through difficult situations to produce a satisfactory outcome for everyone involved. You constantly go out of your way to make others feel appreciated, which is no surprise because you place an exceptionally high value on being accepted and tend to take it personally if someone is rude to you. Famous Allies include Lucille Ball and Johnny Carson.

Strengths:
- Willing to listen
- Working in a team
- Helping others

Challenges:
- Maintaining motivation when working alone
- Tolerating impolite behavior
- Speaking up for yourself

How to make the most of your Ally profile:

- Use your excellent listening skills to help those in need of your support.

- Trust your network. The good relationships you've formed make others willing to go to bat for you.

- Don't be afraid to speak up for yourself. Sometimes being assertive is the only way to solve a problem.

Suggestions for connecting with an Ally:

- Be cautious with your criticism. An Ally will take your comments seriously.

- Need a good idea to help people feel appreciated? Ask an Ally; Allies listen closely to what makes people tick.

- Allies are adept at managing difficult relationships. Let them take the lead when the relationship between two people sours.

The **Architect**

Your ultimate goal is to get some-thing done right, and you have a strong sense of clarity in determining the cor-rect way to complete a task. You are thoughtful and have innovative ideas, while at the same time are analytical and purpose driven. You enjoy a stable,  structured environment and prefer to work with deadlines and clear expectations. You often take plenty of time to analyze information before making a decision, and are willing to delay gratification as long as needed to see things through. George Lucas and Charles Schulz share the Architect profile, as well as 13% of the population.

Strengths:

- Decisions are well thought out
- Having superior organizational skills
- Paying attention to detail

Challenges:

- Focusing on the big picture
- Following your gut
- Tolerating change

How to make the most of your Architect profile:

- Don't be afraid to trust your gut when the situation calls for it.
- Try not to let change take you by surprise; it's often just around the corner.
- Choose tasks where you can clearly see the results from your efforts at each step.

Suggestions for connecting with an Architect:

- Provide an environment where expectations are clearly mapped out, and you follow through on promises.
- Make sure the Architect has enough time to do a task right. Architects emphasize accuracy over meeting a deadline.
- When presenting your case to an Architect, be certain to back it up with good data.

The**Coach**

Your deepest satisfaction comes from helping others to be the best they can. You unflinchingly give your time to develop other people's strengths and help them reach their full potential. You value the long-term, meaningful relationships that build so easily in the  presence of your open-door policy and sympathetic ear. You offer suggestions to problems when asked but ultimately let others make their own decisions. You are trusting and consistently look for and point out the good in others. 9% of the population shares this profile, and famous Coaches include Phil Jackson and Peter Drucker.

Strengths:

- Understanding where others are coming from
- Harnessing the potential in others
- Building camaraderie

Challenges:

- Finding the time to keep projects on task
- Speaking the truth, even when it hurts
- Managing subpar performers

How to make the most of your Coach profile:

- Keep focused on tasks. If you don't, they can easily slip from your radar and reduce your performance.

- Consider criticism to be an attempt to help you develop your strengths. Though other people aren't always as adept at delivering feedback as you are, listening intently to them as you show a thick skin will create a greater sense of trust and cooperation.

- Nonperformers can be a major challenge for you, given your unwillingness to impress your suggestions on others. When dealing with them, seek to understand their perspective before confronting them with inflexible standards.

Suggestions for connecting with a Coach:

- Need a pick-me-up? Talk to a Coach. Coaches are always ready to remind people of their accomplishments.

- A Coach is going to need some gentle prodding to stay focused on tasks, in addition to people.

- A Coach is the ideal person to turn to when you need help resolving challenges and issues in your work.

The Detective

Your thinking is dominated by the use of logic and reason. You tend to focus on the facts because accuracy is the standard by which you evaluate ideas. Your skill in gathering facts and making decisions based on them can serve you well in your career and in life. You  are willing to take the time to get to the bottom of things, no matter how obscured, and expect others to do the same. Your tendency to consider the perspective of others helps you to apply your logic to the big picture, whether it's solving common problems or connecting with others based on ideas that are important to *them*. The Detective profile is not as rare as some people think; it's seen in 9% of the population, including famous problem solvers Thomas Edison and Albert Einstein.

Strengths:

- Emphasizing the bottom line impact of actions
- Gathering data to make sound decisions
- Setting up standards and guidelines

Challenges:

- Admitting mistakes
- Making quick decisions
- Permitting self-disclosure

How to make the most of your Detective profile:

- When a decision needs good research and data to support it, don't hesitate to volunteer your services.
- To develop more trusting and collaborative relationships with others, take opportunities to disclose personal thoughts or feelings about an issue.
- When you've made an error, look to others for information on how you might have made it—seeking knowledge and input from others demonstrates your willingness to acknowledge your mistakes and learn from them.

Suggestions for connecting with a Detective:

- Give a Detective some time to think through the answer to a problem. Detectives need time to consider the data that supports any opinion.
- Include the Detective in developing plans and strategies. A Detective is skilled in anticipating challenges and finding solutions.
- Keep in mind that Detectives are often uncomfortable with the thought of exhibiting flaws in their work.

The Diplomat

You are skilled at relating to almost any personality profile, and people find your style warm and inviting. You focus on respect as the foundation for every relationship. You work hard to make others feel respected, and expect it for yourself. You are most comfort-

able in a stable environment, and place considerable effort into creating and keeping stability in your life. With consistency king, you are not fond of surprises. Famous Diplomats include Desmond Tutu and the Dalai Lama, and Diplomats are seen in 9% of the population.

Strengths:
- Finding a working solution
- Keeping the ball rolling
- Being modest

Challenges:
- Avoiding the crossfire when you're making peace
- Getting the recognition you've earned
- Speaking up for yourself

How to make the most of your Diplomat profile:

- Your modest nature may sometimes prevent others from truly understanding the depth of your experiences. If you don't pass this information on, other people who are unaware of your talents and knowledge may overlook you when it comes to new and challenging opportunities.

- As you work through tasks, ask others if they've found quicker, but just as effective, ways for accomplishing the same result. If you take an effective shortcut, you will have even more time to dedicate to another project of your choice.

- Choose tasks that have consistent, measurable outcomes.

Suggestions for connecting with a Diplomat:

- Diplomats are good-natured and cordial, and they enjoy connecting with many different personality types.

- A Diplomat will prefer consistent and controlled progress in the pursuit of goals, over *any* surprise twists and turns.

- If you want to know what people are thinking and feeling, ask a Diplomat. Diplomats tend to keep a finger on the pulse of group opinion.

The **Entrepreneur**

Your energy comes from pushing boundaries and taking things to the next level. You bore quickly and are drawn to variety. When things are exciting and fresh, you experience a rush of energy that you consider your optimal state. You push yourself hard to reach goals  of all types, and you expect others to do the same. You value independence and control over your environment beyond most other things, and are willing to be bold and sometimes forceful when you really believe in something. Entrepreneurs are 7% of the population, and their most famous members include César Chávez and Bill Gates.

Strengths:

- Focusing on end results
- Ability to "push the envelope"
- Taking control

Challenges:

- Working with a team
- Showing restraint
- Being patient

How to make the most of your Entrepreneur profile:

- People often will have difficulty understanding why you need to move so quickly. Taking the time to explain your motivation to others will go a long way toward feeling understood.

- Accept the reality that you will rarely be deeply satisfied with what you've done. It's your nature to seek a new challenge as soon as the previous one is complete.

- Challenge yourself by finding the moments that require patience. If you treat patience as a challenge required to take advantage of certain opportunities, you will be more likely to demonstrate it.

Suggestions for connecting with an Entrepreneur:

- Remember that Entrepreneurs like to be busy and can even enjoy grinding through a tough project to see it to its end.

- Entrepreneurs have to rack up points each day to feel successful. Be aware of this, as you may notice them keeping track.

- Be quick to praise an Entrepreneur, especially when they go the extra mile on a project, such as showing up early or putting in extra hours. Entrepreneurs like having their efforts noticed.

The **Expert**

You are very knowledgeable in many areas and enjoy discussing and debating topics of interest. You love to learn and work fervently to improve yourself. You are also your toughest critic, and do a good job of keeping yourself on task and making sure you produce

quality work on time. People consider you a perfectionist, but find you casual and coolheaded in social settings. Just 6% of the population are Experts. Jane Goodall and George Washington Carver are famous examples of this personality type.

Strengths:
- Picking things up quickly
- Solving problems
- Being self-motivated

Challenges:
- Recognizing the contributions of others
- Avoiding appearing judgmental
- Not being too hard on yourself

How to make the most of your Expert profile:

- People see you as the resident expert because of your interest in facts and information. They turn to you for all kinds of answers, so don't be too hard on yourself when you don't have them.

- Take a chance on someone else's learning and delegate new responsibility to them. This will build trust and accountability.

- Your desire to demonstrate technical mastery in your work sometimes clouds others' contributions. Find opportunities to publicly or privately recognize others for their contributions to a project or task.

Suggestions for connecting with an Expert:

- Don't be afraid to task an Expert with the challenge of developing knowledge in a new topic or field. Experts strive to be in the know and will go to great lengths to learn as much as possible about a new area.

- Experts have high standards for their personal performance and will judge others by their self-discipline for reaching the same high standards.

- Have the Expert develop a system for storing and sharing the knowledge he or she accumulates.

The**Innovator**

Your energy comes from getting those creative juices flowing. You adapt to change well and have a vision for the future and the way things should be. You are constantly thinking of new ways to look at and interpret things, but you see them through to the end.  You aren't afraid to challenge the status quo, and lose motivation when you can't do things your way. You share the Innovator profile with just 3% of the population, and famous Innovators include Elvis Presley and Pablo Picasso.

Strengths:

- Jumping easily from one task to another
- Making new ideas work
- Being energized by creativity

Challenges:

- Resisting impulsivity
- Fighting boredom
- Demonstrating sympathy

How to make the most of your Innovator profile:

- Avoid projects that require routine or mundane activity.
- Challenge yourself to connect with people who are very different from you, even if you don't necessarily like them.
- When offering coworkers feedback, consider your tone and method of delivery. Focus on blending emotion with professionalism, i.e., kindness or empathy with objective criticism.

Suggestions for connecting with an Innovator:

- Don't be alarmed by the rush of energy Innovators display in response to a new idea or concept that excites them.
- Make sure Innovators have a chance to use their creativity. Keep an open mind to their tendency to develop new ways of doing things.
- When working in a project team, Innovators sometimes compromise interpersonal relationships for the drive to realize their uniqueness and high standards. If you choose to discuss this behavior with them, it's best to do so privately.

The **Mobilizer**

Your outgoing, friendly nature makes it easy for people to follow your lead. You take a genuine interest in those around you and people appreciate it. You like to push yourself and participate in challenging tasks, and often reach your goals. Why? You possess an underly-  ing optimism in the face of adversity that helps you to overcome challenges. Your profile is rare, with just 3% of the population typed as Mobilizers. Famous figures that share your type include Oprah Winfrey and John F. Kennedy.

Strengths:
- Selling (whether it's ideas, products, or services)
- Making things fun
- Being confident

Challenges:
- Confiding in the wrong people
- Getting stuck in static, routine environments
- Lacking decisiveness

How to make the most of your Mobilizer profile:

- Your optimism and enthusiasm are welcome most everywhere. Don't be afraid to show them.

- Your outspoken style, combined with your open and people-oriented manner, can be used effectively to win the position of authority you desire.

- When leading a new project, gather data and facts to support your plan. This will bolster your credibility and help the next time you need to sell a big idea.

Suggestions for connecting with a Mobilizer:

- Mobilizers have an inspiring, persuasive personality that makes them ideal to push others to reach desired objectives. Be sure to provide this opportunity where you can.

- Mobilizers are particularly skilled in opening dialogue with new team members, customers, or potential clients and persuading them to work with you.

- Because of their desire to trust others, Mobilizers can become indecisive during situations that are particularly stressful. You'll need to press them to gather their perspective here.

The **Motivator**

You are sociable and charming and your "people skills" easily win people over. In difficult situations you are motivated by the desire to produce a satisfactory outcome for everyone involved, and you often reach this goal via your ability to speak to the needs of

different perspectives. You place a high value on being liked by others, so naysayers are quick to dominate your attention. The Motivator is one of the most common profiles, as it is shared by 13% of the population. Famous Motivators include Ronald Reagan and Jesse Jackson.

Strengths:
- Bringing people together
- Demonstrating verbal skills
- Having charisma

Challenges:
- Setting limits with other people
- Managing your time
- Dealing with naysayers

How to make the most of your Motivator profile:

- Because of your sociability and charm, people are quick to view you as a friend. Don't be surprised when new acquaintances react this way.

- Build momentum around a task or project by using your well-developed verbal skills to initiate team members and welcome them onboard.

- People are motivated to work with you because of your natural instincts for knowing what drives them. Pay attention to the needs of your team members and use that understanding to foster loyalty.

Suggestions for connecting with a Motivator:

- Motivators are both affable and easy to flatter. Don't hold back your enthusiasm and affection.

- When team members aren't getting along, a Motivator and an Ally will make a good team to lead the group to resolution.

- When other people confuse you, ask a Motivator for guidance. The Motivator's insight will likely help you to understand where the other people are coming from.

The **Opportunist**

You are independent and like to be innovative in your work. You won't let anything stand in your way of getting the job done right and on time. Your focus on personal accountability is fierce, and it's no surprise, then, that you set the same high standards for  others. One of the rarest profiles, you share this type with just 2% of the population. Famous Opportunists include Teddy Roosevelt and Henry Ford, who were known for their hard work, self-reliance, innovation, and willingness to buck the system.

Strengths:

- Coming up with solutions on your own
- Problem-solving with ingenuity
- Meeting deadlines

Challenges:

- Working collaboratively
- Respecting traditions
- Dealing with routine

How to make the most of your Opportunist profile:

- Take the time to recognize the contributions of others. When you don't, your self-reliance can alienate people whose efforts are valuable.

- Your vigorous drive for results can make you inattentive to quality control. Seek support from detail-oriented individuals who can help you monitor the various quality points of a project.

- Pursue tasks that challenge you to use creative problem-solving but are light on routines.

Suggestions for connecting with an Opportunist:

- Opportunists will often shy away from group activities, preferring to work on projects or problems on their own. Give them some room to utilize this tendency.

- Opportunists will seldom rely on traditional methods for problem-solving and are energized by the discovery of creative ways to address a challenge.

- Opportunists are a good choice to help a project team meet a deadline because they can see through barriers that might otherwise hold a group back.

The**Researcher**

As a Researcher, most of what you do is characterized by an utter reliance on logic and reason to solve problems, and a steadfast willingness to complete a project to the end without loose ends. You possess an unusual amount of determination and are highly task fo-

cused. You don't mind working alone to accomplish goals, and are steadfast in your beliefs about what works and what doesn't work. Just 4% of the population share this profile, including famous data hounds Warren Buffett and Jonas Salk.

Strengths:
- Completing tasks to the end without loose ends
- Using logic and reason
- Being confident

Challenges:
- Displaying emotion
- Trusting your gut
- Accepting change

How to make the most of your Researcher profile:

- Because of your low-key and steady nature, others may interpret your style as cold or uncaring. You can avoid this by explaining your passion for facts and objective information.

- Logic and reason appeal to you more than emotion and feelings, so you should pursue tasks that require focus on data and analytical reasoning to interpret problems and devise solutions.

- People see you as rational and thorough, so don't be surprised when they come to you to test their, or someone else's, thinking. Be careful not to deliver your feedback too harshly, or it will deter people from seeking you out.

Suggestions for connecting with a Researcher:

- When presenting an idea or opinion to a Researcher, be sure to support your position with solid data.

- Researchers require clearly stated goals and an organized plan to work effectively on a project.

- You will have far better luck winning over a Researcher with logical reasoning than you will with displays of emotion.

The **Sponsor**

You develop friendships with ease and value knowing lots of people from all walks of life. You like to connect other people for work and social purposes, and enjoy building your own network as well. You sometimes find yourself lost in conversation and enjoy showing your

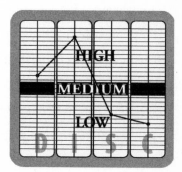

appreciation for those around you. You actively seek opportunities to socialize, leading you to a variety of informal social groups. The Sponsor is the most common profile, though it's still shared by just 16% of the population. Famous Sponsors include George Burns and Shaquille O'Neal.

Strengths:

- Showing public appreciation for the work of others
- Being adept at all forms of communication
- Promoting harmony with others

Challenges:

- Getting lost in conversations
- Overcommitting yourself
- Following through

How to make the most of your Sponsor profile:

- You enjoy talking to others and search for these opportunities, sometimes compromising your focus on a certain task or project.
- Don't underestimate how easily you create friendships and contacts through your outgoing, friendly style. This is a trait that others appreciate.
- You have the tendency to promise to complete certain tasks that are beyond what is realistic given your schedule. Keep track of these promises to ensure that you don't take on too much. This will build trust and reliability in the eyes of others.

Suggestions for connecting with a Sponsor:

- Be generous with your praise. Sponsors love to know their work is appreciated.
- Sponsors are readily accepted into different social circles and are an easy addition to a new group.
- A Sponsor's optimism is welcome during the stress-filled moments of tension that inevitably surface in groups.

The **Strategist**

You are adept at planning and creating a path for people to follow. You are painstaking in your strategies and have an uncanny ability to think a few steps ahead. This helps alleviate headaches for those around you because they know that nine times out of ten your plan will work. As a Strategist, you are the rarest of breeds, with just 1% of the population sharing this profile. Famous Strategists include George S. Patton and Vince Lombardi.

Strengths:

- Finding a workable solution
- Devising a clear plan of action
- Earning the trust of those you work with

Challenges:

- Delivering constructive criticism
- Lacking patience
- Fearing failure

How to make the most of your Strategist profile:

- In your desire to take advantage of an exciting new route to move things forward, you may appear restless or impatient to others. When you feel pressure to quicken the pace, stop and check in with others on this.
- Your predominantly collaborative work style is well received, and with your critical thinking ability, you are adept at creating competitive, successful teams.
- Sometimes your competitiveness is manifested in sharp criticism of others that does more to weaken than strengthen them.

Suggestions for connecting with a Strategist:

- Strategists are keenly aware of the unique perspectives in any group, and they are good at using this knowledge to win everyone's involvement in the task at hand.
- When facing tough problems, Strategists are often thinking several steps ahead. In a disagreement, stop to make sure the two of you are talking about the same thing.
- Only 1 in 100 people has the Strategist profile. If you have one in your team, take advantage of the Strategist's unique visionary ability.

5: Managing the Fourteen Types

LISE HAS WORKED in some challenging environments in her career, but the nine weeks she spent on a quarter-acre lump of sand out in the western Pacific, some seven hundred miles from civilization, clearly takes the cake. Working in a team of seven marine biologists, they spent their days studying the endangered Hawaiian monk seal, and their nights in the remains of an abandoned coast guard barracks. For more than two months, their only form of communication with the outside world was an antediluvian two-way radio. Like most every other working group, the team had a manager who was responsible for setting its direction. And just like every other team, this direction had little to do with tasks. The manager's job was to keep the members of the team working well together as a cohesive group. Successful managers don't leave this process to chance. And to hear Elise tell the story, the potential for conflict among members of the team was scarier than the time she was chased from the water by a twelve-foot tiger shark. "Being in the sun all day observing animals that feared us—surrounded by their predators that could easily kill or maim us—and then having to work into the evening cleaning, managing, and protecting our equipment . . . relationship stuff sometimes went by the wayside." The most formidable challenges weren't the heat exhaustion, the threat of an impending tidal wave, or trying to ensure the survival of a tiny seal pup that had lost a flipper to a hungry shark. Adversity came in working alongside the same faces each day within the confines of the island. "It all came down to realizing it was just us and nobody else. Only by leaning on the shared goals, recognizing the human side of our experience, and finding commonality could we face the conflicts that popped up. Having such a great coach there to guide us made all the difference."

Conflict among people is an inevitable part of work, and—like the ominous shark fin surfacing in the distance—its presence has warning signs. Successful managers beat the odds by heeding these signs, looking within their group, and striving to understand the various personalities sitting at the table. Understanding the members of your team does more than help you avoid conflict; it helps you use the strengths of each to achieve the greatest results possible. As we learned in Chapter 2, people don't naturally develop an objective understanding of their strengths. A manager who educates and understands her team has a powerful and enduring influence upon the success of the group. Given short deadlines and stacked schedules, how can a manager accomplish this? The first step is to assess the personality of each member of your team. (Since none of the fourteen personality types is better than any other, this process should be received by your team without too much hesitation.) Learn the profile of each team member, studying the principal characteristics that define each person's type (see Chapter 4). Even in a highly specialized job function, a team is unlikely to be composed of more than two individuals who share the same personality profile. If you have a team of seven individuals or more, you'll probably have to learn a minimum of five profiles (on average it's four profiles for every five team members). The strategies outlined in the remainder of this chapter will walk you through the specifics of managing each of the fourteen personality profiles. Unless you have a small team, this information is far more than you can retain on a single pass, so it's formatted in bulleted lists that make it easy for you to come back and reference it as needed.

The strategies outlined for each personality type will help you to do two important things. First, they'll help you relate to each team member, based upon the personality traits that dictate the bulk of his behavior. These strategies will assist you every day, but are especially critical during times of high stress when people become inflexible as they seek refuge in a narrow repertoire that relies heavily on their fixed personalities. Your job is to recognize this phenomenon and understand what motivates this sometimes inscrutable behavior. A manager is only effective when he can address team members constructively and directly. People will follow your direction only when they feel understood.

The second major insight you'll gain regards the roles for which each of the fourteen personality types is best suited. You'll learn how to utilize the unique strengths of each team member to drive the success of the entire group forward. These strategies focus on the actual position in which the person works, the roles you assign to help the group complete a task, and the traits you can rely on to motivate each individually in the group to synergy and cooperation.

The chart on page 86 lists each of the fourteen personality types and indicates the general tendency of people to rely more or less on each of the four DISC personality traits, depending on their type. Photocopy this chart, or download it from this book's website (www.personalitycode .com), highlight the profiles of your team members, and keep it handy as a snapshot of your team. After all, your job is to take care of your team—to help each member be as effective as possible in his or her work.

Who in my team?		DOMINANT	INTERPERSONAL	STEADY	CONSCIENTIOUS
	ALLY	LESS	MORE	MORE	LESS
	ARCHITECT	LESS	LESS	MORE	MORE
	COACH	LESS	MORE	MORE	LESS
	DETECTIVE	LESS	LESS	LESS	MORE
	DIPLOMAT	LESS	VARIED	MORE	LESS
	ENTREPRENEUR	MORE	LESS	LESS	LESS
	EXPERT	LESS	MORE	LESS	MORE
	INNOVATOR	MORE	LESS	LESS	MORE
	MOBILIZER	MORE	MORE	LESS	MORE
	MOTIVATOR	MORE	MORE	LESS	LESS
	OPPORTUNIST	MORE	LESS	VARIED	LESS
	RESEARCHER	LESS	LESS	MORE	LESS
	SPONSOR	LESS	MORE	LESS	LESS
	STRATEGIST	VARIED	MORE	LESS	MORE

Use this chart to build a snapshot of the personalities on your team, and keep it handy to use as a quick reference. The columns illustrate whether people with each profile tend to rely more or less on each of the four DISC personality traits. Because this table is a quick reference, it does not capture every variation seen in the fourteen personality types. To fine-tune your understanding of your team, ask people to share their IDISC report with you, and take note of how high, moderate, or low they are in each personality trait.

How to Manage an Ally

- The Ally will have difficulty maintaining motivation when working alone. Remember that this isn't an issue of work ethic but, rather, a product of the energy he derives from being in the presence of other people. The Ally's fondness for working in groups is essential to his well-being. Keep this in mind when choosing tasks for him.

- The Ally has an unusual ability to discern what is truly important to people and listen in a way that few others can. As a result the Ally collects all kinds of information on what other people really care about. Need a good idea to help someone feel appreciated? Consider asking your local Ally for ideas.

- Be cautious when delivering feedback. An Ally is more apt to take your suggestions as criticism than most other personality types. The trick is to be selective about what you say—as an Ally will take everything you say very seriously.

- If you live and/or work with an Ally, remember that Allies can have trouble speaking up for themselves. Sometimes this may be obvious to you, but other times you'll find yourself frustrated with your Ally and not even realize (without thinking about it) that there is something the Ally is not telling you. This isn't intentional. It's just the result of the Ally's tendency to put the needs of other people ahead of his own. A little help with speaking up can go a long way at the right moment.

- Brash and rude behavior rubs the Ally raw because it is antithetical to his deepest values. So don't be surprised if an Ally takes it very seriously—and personally.

How to Manage an Architect

- The Architect needs specific deadlines and clear expectations in order to work effectively. Her ultimate goal is to get something done right, and she needs clarity to help her determine the correct way to complete a task. The Architect will achieve optimal performance in a stable, structured environment.

- An Architect is good at delaying gratification, which is a rare skill that you can call upon as the situation requires it. Even though she is thoughtful and creative in her thinking, she is analytical and purpose-driven enough to see things through when the going gets tough.

- Architects are excellent at ensuring the optimization of operational policies and procedures, as well as compliance with established standards and regulations. If an Architect isn't already working in an operations or compliance function, she is well-suited to stretch her skills and try an assignment in these departments.

- Architects emphasize accuracy over meeting a deadline. Make sure the Architect has enough time to do a task right.

- In managing an Architect, it is very important that you follow through on your promises. Failing to do so will erode her trust in you.

- An Architect's biggest challenge is learning to trust her gut. Since every decision can't be as well thought out as she may wish, you'll likely have to work closely with her and actively manage her performance to ensure that she is able to trust her gut in situations that offer no other option.

How to Manage a Coach

- A Coach's deepest satisfaction comes from helping others to be the best they can. Find opportunities for him to fully realize this, such as creating a mentoring program or an orientation program for new team members.

- A Coach tends to prefer group activities and will be most effective with the fewest independent tasks.

- Just as a Coach is motivated to harness the potential in others, his own professional growth is also a high priority. Support his participation in professional associations and professional development programs. The time and dollars he expends attending these events is well spent.

- A Coach will give unflinchingly of his time to develop other people's strengths and help them reach their full potential. His open-door policy and sympathetic ear can make it difficult for him to get other work done. You'll likely have to keep a watchful eye on this and coach him through keeping it from wreaking havoc on his schedule.

- Coaches who are managers often have difficulty handling non-performers. A Coach is not inclined to impress his suggestions on others, and he likes to see people take responsibility for their work. If this is the case, you'll likely need to coach your Coach through techniques for addressing the nonperformers he supervises.

How to Manage a Detective

- A Detective is ready and willing to take the time needed to explore the facts—no matter how obscured—and get to the bottom of an issue. This is an unusual skill that you should call on when the situation requires it.

- When you deliver feedback to a Detective, keep in mind that she is highly uncomfortable with the thought of exhibiting flaws in her work. Her utter reliance on logic and reason doesn't make for a comfortable conversation when this logic fails. You will be better off exploring future strategies for improving her fact-gathering and decision-making than you will be if you dwell on her mistakes.

- A Detective is well suited to be included in the development of plans and strategies. She is skilled in anticipating challenges and finding solutions. Letting her join project or strategic planning sessions is a great stretch assignment that can help her improve her leadership skills.

- A Detective is most effective when she completes some tasks in groups and others independently. The Detective's biggest need for working alone comes from her desire to gather facts before forming a solid opinion. When she explores an issue with the rest of her team, she'll often want to conduct some research independently and then return this information to the group in subsequent discussions.

- A Detective is not prone to self-disclosure, which can make her come across a bit standoffish to other team members. You'll have to watch for this and coach her through sharing more to win favor with the rest of the team.

How to Manage a Diplomat

- Sometimes when you want to know what a Diplomat is thinking, you're just going to have to ask. When the Diplomat thinks that keeping his opinion to himself promotes harmony, that's what he'll do. If you ask him for his thoughts, he'll usually tell you, because it isn't in the spirit of cooperation not to do so.

- A Diplomat will prefer consistent and controlled progress in the pursuit of goals. If you want to get the most from a Diplomat, assign him tasks that have consistent, measurable outcomes and a low likelihood of unexpected twists and turns.

- If you want to know what team members are thinking and feeling, ask a Diplomat. He is skilled at relating to most any personality profile, and his team members find his style warm and inviting. He's a good listener, who is genuinely interested in what others have to say, and he tends to keep a finger on the pulse of group opinion.

- A Diplomat will need your coaching and support to stand up for himself and get the recognition his work deserves. This is especially critical for Diplomats in earlier stages of their careers. Without your support, the Diplomat's modest nature is likely to prevent others from understanding the nature of his talents and the depth of his knowledge and experience, to the detriment of the team's performance.

- A Diplomat does not like surprises. Don't spring things on him if you want to earn his support. When you need a Diplomat to make a decision with long-term implications for his career, be certain to give him ample time to contemplate the best course of action.

How to Manage an Entrepreneur

- An Entrepreneur's energy comes from pushing boundaries and taking things to previously unseen levels. This ensures that she bores quickly and is drawn to variety in her work. Assign tasks accordingly and you will see the rush of energy that comes from her optimal state.

- The Entrepreneur's boundary pushing can lead to trouble if it goes unchecked. You might have to step in at times to help the Entrepreneur understand when she's taking on too much risk.

- Be quick to praise an Entrepreneur, especially when she goes the extra mile on a project, such as showing up early or putting in extra hours. An Entrepreneur likes having her efforts noticed, and she has to rack up points each day to feel successful.

- The Entrepreneur is bold and charismatic when she believes in something. This quality can make for a highly successful salesperson.

- Restraint and patience are not the Entrepreneur's strong suits. Coworkers will have difficulty understanding why she needs to move so quickly.

- Whenever people are convinced that something "can't be done," the Entrepreneur is just dying to prove them wrong. This translates to a willingness to see things through that others find incredibly difficult, and it's a great way for the Entrepreneur to make a unique contribution to the group.

How to Manage an Expert

- Don't be afraid to give an Expert the challenge of developing knowledge in a new topic or field. An Expert will pick things up quickly. However, an Expert will also tend to be hard on herself, which can make her resistant to immersing herself in an unfamiliar area. Your job is to ensure that these assignments are provided, which puts her excellent problem-solving skills to work outside of a single, narrow discipline.

- An Expert is her toughest critic. She loves to learn and will work fervently to improve herself. You'll have to work a little harder when delivering feedback to make certain she really hears you and understands how much these efforts are appreciated.

- An Expert often has difficulty with delegating. Her desire for technical mastery in her work can stifle others' contributions, as she doesn't want to take the risk of letting someone else complete the task. When this happens, make delegating part of her assignment and manage her performance to see that it happens. This will build trust and accountability with her teammates.

- People often turn to the Expert for answers, because they know she is a source for facts and information. Have the Expert develop a system for storing and sharing the knowledge she accumulates.

- Even though the Expert is a perfectionist, she is casual and cool-headed in social settings. She loathes conflict so much that she will err on the side of passivity when issues should be addressed. Coach her through addressing people assertively when the situation calls for it, so that she doesn't allow herself to be stepped on.

How to Manage an Innovator

- An Innovator's energy skyrockets when he is able to get those creative juices flowing. Assign tasks that require him to find new ways of understanding and interpreting things, and you'll reap the benefits from this incredible rush of energy.

- Innovators often have difficulty seeing eye to eye with team members of opposing personalities, and this can quickly escalate to the point that you'll have to step in and manage his performance. When this happens, challenge the Innovator to find ways to connect with teammates who see the world differently from him, and then hold him accountable for doing so.

- An Innovator can easily jump from one task to another, so you can rely on him to switch to a new project when other team members are hesitant.

- Avoid assigning projects to the Innovator that require routine or mundane activity. He is easily bored by these tasks, and will lack the energy needed to do them well.

- An Innovator can work well alone, and is usually better off spending his time this way. It's easy for him to lose motivation if he's always having to consider the team's concerns.

- Challenge the Innovator to accept patience as an important component of the creative process. Otherwise he'll have more trouble harmonizing with the rest of the team.

- When delivering feedback to an Innovator, you will have better luck offering suggestions than you will corrections. He tends to vigorously defend his ideas.

How to Manage a Mobilizer

- Mobilizers have an inspiring personality that makes them ideal to push others to reach desired objectives. Utilize this powerful skill as much as possible.

- The Mobilizer has a unique ability to match people up on the basis of complementary needs. Her perspective and enthusiasm for connecting people is a valuable tool that can move a project, or any important endeavor, forward.

- You'll find a Mobilizer is one of the last people to nitpick others over trivial details. Don't let her brush over the facts when the team needs good data to support her own opinions. In many situations her colleagues will not be satisfied with her suggestions unless she can provide some data to support her stance.

- A Mobilizer is quick to trust others. While this is generally effective, it can also be her biggest Achilles' heel. She'll need help learning when is the right time to pull back and prevent putting her trust in the wrong person.

- A Mobilizer's outgoing, friendly nature makes it easy for people to follow her lead. A Mobilizer tends to make an active, involved leader because she blends her outspoken style with an open and people-oriented attitude.

- A Mobilizer is most effective when her schedule has a good balance between group and independent activities. Make certain you provide these opportunities.

- A Mobilizer likes to push herself and participate in challenging tasks—don't be afraid to challenge her.

How to Manage a Motivator

- The Motivator is a persuasive personality with abundant "people skills." He can easily win people over with his charisma and verbal mastery, which makes him a good choice for any task that requires selling. Understand that these skills aren't just useful for sales in the traditional sense—the Motivator can provide a compelling argument anytime people need to be convinced of something.

- Putting artificial constraints on a Motivator's time and schedule is a sure way to alienate him from his work. The Motivator works best when he has a good measure of control over when and how he gets things done.

- When giving feedback to a Motivator, remember that he places a high value on being accepted. He can take corrective criticism, but you'll need to be cautious about making him feel like you don't trust his judgment or are questioning the quality of his character.

- Motivators tend to keep a finger on the pulse of the unique perspectives evident in their team. Be sure to mine this data, as you can use this understanding of the team to know what drives them and foster loyalty.

- Motivators are allergic to data and in-depth analysis. You'll get the most from a Motivator if you help him keep such tasks out of his schedule.

- Motivators are so enthusiastic and complimentary that people can easily think they don't need to return the favor. Be generous with your praise and don't hide your enthusiasm; a Motivator is both affable and easy to flatter.

How to Manage an Opportunist

- An Opportunist is a creative thinker who doesn't let obstacles stop her from getting things done. The Opportunist's focus on accountability is fierce, which makes her a great lead on projects that have critical schedules.

- When delegating to an Opportunist, you won't need to spend as much time explaining *how* things need to be done as you do with most other profiles. An Opportunist usually finds her own creative ways to solve problems, so your time should be spent convincing her of *why* a task is important. Then let her put her creativity to work in making it happen.

- Opportunists are often misunderstood. Other team members may find them pushy because it's easy to mistake their drive for performance as single-minded or even self-centered thinking. Your job is to help the Opportunist understand this, and explain her motives to the team.

- An Opportunist will often shy away from group activities, preferring to work on projects or problems on her own. If you want peak performance from members of your team possessing this profile, make sure you leave her room to do so.

- An Opportunist will buck the system and challenge the status quo. She is highly skeptical of traditions and routine. Keep the lines of communication open with her to ensure that this energy is well directed. If you don't, you may find that the system she is bucking is your own.

- An Opportunist will seldom rely on traditional methods for problem-solving and is energized by the discovery of creative ways to address a challenge. Assign tasks that are less confining and challenge her to use creative problem-solving.

How to Manage a Researcher

- Don't expect quick decisions from a Researcher—he needs time to collect the facts before he is comfortable offering an opinion.

- Be cautious about putting him in a position where he has to constantly react to change. A Researcher performs best in a steady, stable environment.

- When it comes to persistence, a Researcher is often going to be a project team's backbone. Researchers possess an unusual amount of tenacity and want to see tasks completed without loose ends.

- Be sure to provide opportunities for the Researcher to demonstrate his expertise. Such opportunities are an extremely motivating and rewarding part of his work.

- Researchers require clearly stated goals and an organized work plan in order to be their best. Keep this in mind anytime you delegate to him, as well as when you are soliciting his support for an initiative.

- When you have a Researcher who is underperforming or needs to develop a new skill, work with him to develop a detailed action plan that captures the specific steps he needs to take in order to fulfill this requirement. Ask for regular progress reports that allow him to bring you data on the actions taken and the changes being made.

- It's easy for other members of the team to see the Researcher as cold or uncaring, because of his low-key and steady nature. You may have to coach him through explaining his passion for facts and information to the rest of the team.

- When presenting an idea or opinion to a Researcher, be sure to support your position with solid data. You will have far better luck winning over a Researcher with logic and reason than you will with charismatic displays of emotion.

How to Manage a Sponsor

- The Sponsor is motivated more by people than by achievement. This means she'll be more enthusiastic and productive when working in a team that has good camaraderie than one that doesn't get along, even if it's handling an important assignment.

- A Sponsor can have the tendency to overpromise, and say that she can complete tasks that are unrealistic in light of her schedule. This is an important area for you to help a Sponsor and manage her performance. You'll need to create accountability for her in saying no to others when her plate is already full.

- A Sponsor makes an easy addition to an existing group. She is highly social and outgoing, ensuring that she is readily accepted into a variety of circles.

- A Sponsor feels bogged down by mundane tasks and gravitates toward conversations that are easy for her to get lost in. This can distract a Sponsor from optimal performance, as all jobs require some amount of mundane activity. You'll need to help her build awareness of this quality, set clear expectations for her work, and manage her performance to ensure that mundane tasks are completed.

- When providing feedback to a Sponsor, be generous with your praise. She loves to know that her work is appreciated.

- A Sponsor is highly flexible in the face of change, and is good at seeing the bright side of an about-face. She is well suited for positions that endure frequent changes, and often creates a contagious enthusiasm that helps others get behind a change.

How to Manage a Strategist

- The Strategist is the rarest of the fourteen personality types—it's seen in just 1% of the population. If you have a Strategist in your team, be sure to put him in a position that capitalizes on his unique visionary ability. For some managers, this ability can be hard to see, especially in an employee that is in the early stages of his career. Remember that even the greatest Strategists have to start somewhere.

- A Strategist is hesitant to speak up and address conflicts with other team members. This can easily lead to problems that fester, and you'll have to step in and coach the Strategist through addressing interpersonal issues assertively before they are blown out of proportion.

- The Strategist is adept at planning and creating a path for others to follow. He is well suited to leadership roles because his uncanny ability to think a few steps ahead alleviates headaches for the rest of the team and earns their trust.

- A Strategist can turn sharply from outgoing and friendly to critical and impatient when he feels like other people are taking advantage of him. As much as a Strategist likes to offer a clear plan of action, he is sensitive to people who rely too heavily on his opinions. You'll have to help a Strategist avoid sharp criticism of others, and your best route to accomplish this comes in explaining to the Strategist that this tendency does more to weaken than strengthen the team.

6: Type vs. Anti-Type

J ANET AND VANESSA epitomized the modern working mother—they were educated, every bit as focused on career as family, and climbing the management ranks inside the same cell phone manufacturer. Both women had a newborn at home, and they planned to work half-time for several months until they were comfortable sending the babies to child care while they were at work. Their company decided to have them split a single management position, each working half-time. On paper, Janet and Vanessa had so much in common that they seemed a perfect match—both were high energy, worked long hours, and had managed a team before with great success. The novelty of the assignment made their first month of splitting the position a lot of fun. Janet was there on Monday and Tuesday, they shared duty on Wednesday, and Vanessa handled things alone on Thursday and Friday.

But after the first month, things began deteriorating rapidly. Janet had previously succeeded by being a sure-footed leader who set clear, ambitious goals for her team and offered them great independence in reaching them. She continued this tactic during her half of the week. Vanessa's style the rest of the week was the polar opposite of Janet's— she was collaborative, highly involved, and essentially nurtured her team to success by working side by side with them. Team members privately referred to Mondays and Tuesdays as "Type A days," Thursdays and Fridays as "Type B days," and Wednesdays as "fight days." And fight they did. Wednesdays became a day for butting heads, as the two managers struggled to reconcile their management styles. Their frustration and resentment grew quickly as each manager believed that *her* perspective was *right*. The conflict alienated their team, stressed both managers out, and didn't leave anyone better for experiencing it. The team's sales at the end of the term were the lowest in the department, and half the volume either manager had previously achieved with her own team.

When Personalities Clash

It's hard to imagine a profession where success is not influenced by the ability to get along with other people. This is especially true with work today, where teamwork is a pervasive element of how things get done. Unfortunately, when you bring a group of people together, conflict is bound to follow, and while some clashes are unavoidable, most are fueled by a simple lack of understanding. Why can't we stay on the same page at work? First, our brains are hardwired to assume that other people's motivations are just like our own. It's natural to assume that my colleagues think like me. If they do something I don't agree with, I'm bound to consider their actions careless, insensitive, or just plain wrong. Too often we fail to consider the impetus for their behavior. It's easier to assume weakness or ill will on their part than it is to stop and discover the motivation behind their actions. When my colleague's personality type is similar to my own—even if it isn't a perfect match—we're far more likely to react the same way to things and think on the same page. As the gap between our personalities widens, our opinions diverge more frequently. Like we saw with Janet and Vanessa, conflict is the inevitable result.

Most of us have at least one person we're always tiptoeing around to avoid a conflict. Ever wonder why certain people can be so difficult to get along with? Chances are, your personality types are a poor match. Each type has a nearly polar opposite that, though it doesn't preclude the two from connecting, it guarantees that understanding each other is going to be a bit of work. It's tempting to throw a wall up when people don't seem to share our motivations and tendencies. And the more disparate the personality types are of any two individuals, the more likely they are to have trouble connecting. In this chapter, I break the fourteen DISC personality types into seven opposing pairs. Each of these type/anti-type pairings brings together two profiles whose core motivations—their essence for being, if you will—are fundamentally opposed. The graph of each personality type's DISC levels—provided at the start of each section—helps illustrate why they clash. By studying the explanations behind the seven type/anti-type pairings, you'll learn why two people can butt heads so easily and how simply conflict can be avoided. The type/anti-type pairings don't necessarily mean that two types will clash, but, rather, the analyses provide a means to understand why they often do. Even better, the pairings are a way to understand which aspects of human character conflict and what can be done to forge a solid connection between them.

Type vs. Anti-Type

Type	Anti-Type
ALLY	OPPORTUNIST
ARCHITECT	SPONSOR
COACH	INNOVATOR
DETECTIVE	MOTIVATOR
DIPLOMAT	ENTREPRENEUR
MOBILIZER	EXPERT
RESEARCHER	STRATEGIST

The pairs of personality types sharing a row have the tendency to clash. The prevailing characteristics of these types are bound to contradict each other, thereby requiring a greater level of understanding between the two people involved. They'll have to work harder to make sense of each other than they will people of any other type.

A llies value the quality of their relationships above all other things. They know that listening is a great way to connect with people, and they've honed this ability in a way that few others have. Those around the Ally are quick to recognize this affinity for the interpersonal, and they rely on his attentive ear when they need support. Enter the Opportunist, a likely source of conflict because he expends far less energy on people. The Opportunist is primarily motivated by the desire for control over his environment—he is task focused, and the needs of other people are secondary to his own goals and interests. When the Opportunist announces that he will be working on a new project alone and doesn't want any help, this has far more to do with a desire for control than a lack of faith in the group. Since the Ally is focused first on the social side of things, the Opportunist's behavior is often perceived as an attack. It's easy to consider it an insult to the group, or an indication that the Opportunist doesn't like his colleagues. The Ally is bound to find this act more offensive than, say, an

Entrepreneur, who is more apt to understand because he shares a similar focus on tasks.

In reality, both approaches have validity, but conflict is created by failing to consider each other's perspective. As an Ally, you can align yourself with the Opportunist by recognizing the importance of the task, regardless of his impatience. For him, the same "aha!" moment that produces a great idea also produces the sensation of missing out on it (he needs to get going *now,* with or without other people). If you're an Ally who is having trouble with this, don't be afraid to lean on others for support. People often refer to you as "nice" because you go out of your way to make everyone feel appreciated, and place an exceptionally high value on being accepted. The result? You are thin-skinned in the face of disregard and criticism. It's far better to be aware of this sensitivity than to deny it when you're clashing with a task-focused personality. Recognizing the feeling when it's coming minimizes its grip on your thinking. Because you go out of your way to make people feel respected and appreciated, you are instinctively irritated by those who do the opposite. The key to developing thicker skin lies in understanding that few people place the same value as you do on treating people well.

As an Ally, whether you are choosing a profession, a hobby, or a mate, you are going to be miserable without the chance to spread your social wings. Why? Though you may also be able to tolerate, and even enjoy, working alone, you have far more difficulty maintaining your motivation in solitary tasks, and this catches up with you. When working in groups, your abundant "people skills" are evident to everyone, and they'll want you to put them to good use. Just don't be afraid to use your alliances; the good relationships you've formed mean that others are willing to go to bat for you.

As an Opportunist, your profile is defined by Dominance, which means the thing you value most is the feeling of being competent and in control. The Ally will often have difficulty understanding why you need to move so quickly, but making things happen at a rabbit's pace not only gives you a sense of control over the process, it also pushes the accepted understanding of how quickly something can be done. If you take the time to explain this motivation to others, they are going to be far more likely to give you the room to be yourself, and at a minimum you'll make some progress in feeling understood. You'll have to be open with an Ally and seek feedback if you want to find out if your actions make him feel frustrated. He won't always agree with the emphasis you place on tasks, and he may even suggest, at times, that your actions hold you back. Let him speak his mind—this in itself is an act of teamwork. And his goal is to assist you by offering advice, not to defeat you. In the end, you can give him a touch of your attention and still stay true to your type. And you must, for your style is not only "as good" as any other—it's often the only way to push our current performance to new heights.

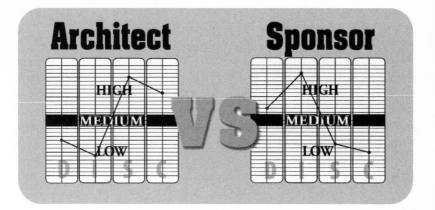

Clashes between the Architect and Sponsor are common, if not for the stark contrast between these types but because there are just so many of them out there. With 16% of the population being Sponsors, and 13% Architects, almost a third of us holds one of these two personality types. And they have very different goals in life. The Architect's sense of purpose comes in getting things done right—she's predominantly Conscientious—while the Sponsor is highly Interpersonal and motivated far more by people than achievement. The Architect is highly analytical and task-focused. She is comfortable in a stable, structured environment where expectations are clear, deadlines are set, and plans are followed. The Sponsor, on the other hand, is all about social interaction. She's jazzed working with other people. It's easy for her to get lost in conversation, but she doesn't sweat it much when deadlines slip. To the Sponsor, deadlines are artificial impositions upon our time—life isn't about what you achieve, it's about the connections you form along the way.

When you put these two on the same team, their conflicting needs tend to rise to the surface, and often wax and wane according to the current priorities of the group. For example, when a team is pushing a deadline, the Sponsor's tendency to get lost in conversation can grate on the Architect in a big way. Deadlines bring a huge focus on tasks to the group, and the Architect's tendency toward planning and structure take precedent. The chatty and social Sponsor can get alienated from the rest of the group by an Architect, whose tendencies suddenly make her the righteous one. And things flip-flop during the downtime. Here the Sponsor's rapport with the rest of the team is well received and great for motivation. Mundane tasks are less important during downtime, and people enjoy the energy she brings to regular meetings. The Architect, on the other hand, has far less interest in these things. She needs specific deadlines and clear expectations to work effectively, so she's already pushing the group to set goals, plan activities, and essentially dive head-first into a big pile of mundane activity. Suddenly the cheery Sponsor is the one getting irritated. Conflict between them erupts, and the situation dictates who seems to be "wrong" for following her natural tendencies.

The key for bringing the Sponsor and Architect together is segmenting their work. I'm not suggesting they don't work together. They just need to understand whose job it is to do which task. Even under the incredible pressure of a deadline, a team needs some social reprieve. If an Architect understands that a Sponsor is going to be the one to provide this, she shouldn't be so frustrated when the Sponsor acts on the impulse. Likewise, planning is important to the success of the group. When teams don't set a course for themselves to follow, they usually end up scratching their heads in the end, looking back and wondering what happened. The Architect's drive for planning and structure is the key to the Sponsor and the rest of the team having clear expectations for their work. While the Architect's nerdy tendency for planning is frustrating to the Sponsor, it's what ensures that the mundane tasks—that the Sponsor will otherwise let slip by the wayside—are completed on time.

Some of the DISC type/anti-type combinations are better off in a boss/subordinate relationship. This isn't the case for the Architect and Sponsor, who fare far better as peers. The biggest reason to keep them on the same level is that their goals are impossible to reconcile. You see, the perfect boss is one who understands her tendencies and interests and separates them from the requirements she sets for *your* job. But how often does this happen? In the real world, your boss's priorities for your work are tainted by her own motivations. In the case of the Architect and Sponsor, their needs are so opposed that it's easy for this to create conflict. The Sponsor develops friendships with such ease that one of her biggest professional strengths comes in her network. She builds her network via seeking opportunities to socialize with people from all walks of life. When the Sponsor's boss is an Architect, her focus is far more on tasks than on people. She evaluates her employees' performance according to their ability to plan well and complete mundane tasks on schedule. These are not the Sponsor's strengths. Sponsors have the tendency to overpromise and say that they can complete tasks that are unrealistic in light of their schedule. While this can distract a Sponsor from optimal performance, the error is magnified when she works for an Architect. If you are a Sponsor working for an Architect, the biggest and most realistic change you can make is to follow through on your promises to your boss. Failure to do so can quickly erode her trust in you. The flip side of the equation—an Architect with a Sponsor for a boss—creates problems that are a bit more subtle. The Sponsor is less likely to be deeply frustrated by the Architect's desire to plan and focus on tasks. Most people consider this a more fundamental element of a job, so it's hard to be critical of it. Plus, Sponsors don't tend to be rigid with other people. They're fairly curious about what makes people tick, which makes them more accepting of how their employees "choose" to approach their work.

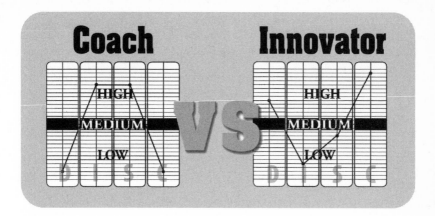

The personality profiles of the Coach and Innovator couldn't be any more different. These polar opposites are in starker contrast than any of the other type/anti-type pairs. Tremendous amounts of conflict—or synergy—are the result. When you put the Coach's and Innovator's graphs side by side, the antithesis is easy to see—they look like the other's graph flipped over. The Innovator is quick to act, open to change, and likes to be in control, where the Coach is patient, easygoing, and in need of stability. Where the Coach derives his energy from people and loves to work in groups, the Innovator is primarily interested in tasks and needs to spend much of his time working alone. The Innovator doesn't believe in making things right—he believes in making them perfect. The Coach's interest in the details is moderate at best.

The Coach and Innovator are unique enough that you'll often see them operating on different planes. Like aircraft passing in the night, they might not collide, but if they do it's a disaster. And feedback is usually the place where the Coach and Innovator crash. The Coach's deepest satisfaction comes from helping others to be the best they can. He unflinchingly gives his time to develop other people's strengths and help them reach their full potential, but he does this without telling them what to do. The Coach believes that people should choose their own course; his resistance to offer opinions is how he shows respect. The Innovator is task-focused—his energy comes from acting quickly in response to creative tension. He is first to speak his mind and challenge the status quo. The Innovator is constantly looking for new ways to look at and interpret things, and relies on this exploration as a source of inspiration. Since the Innovator isn't focused primarily on people, it's easy for him to say things that, at best, lack tact and, at worst, don't adequately consider the perspective of the other person. This is a sore spot for the otherwise easygoing Coach. To him, such direct or abrasive feedback is a tremendous sign of disrespect.

Another source of fuel for the fire is the Coach's resistance to confrontation. Since he isn't quick to offer feedback or tell people what he thinks, he'll tend to sit on this perceived disrespect until things get ugly. By the time the Innovator hears about it, feelings are in the way. Like most personality clashes, the solution for the Coach and Innovator lies in communication. The Innovator is sensitive to criticism but concerned with improvement. If the Coach finds something that the Innovator does uncomfortable, it's time for him to speak up for himself sooner—not later. If the Coach can share what the Innovator's actions *feel like to him* and specifically request that he do things differently, the Innovator is likely to consider this improvement. The only change for the Coach here is to speak up. His knack for seeing the good in others and offering suggestions, but letting them make their own decisions, will keep the Innovator from feeling resistant when criticized.

Just as the Coach needs to speak up for himself to work effectively with his anti-type, the Innovator needs to demonstrate patience with people and understand that teamwork is an important component of the creative process. Teamwork (whether in the form of a family bike ride, PTA meeting, or in the boardroom) by nature requires a great deal of patience, empathy, and release of control. As an Innovator, would you be better off living in a cave? Absolutely not. You just need to recognize that most group activities are going to require some extra energy and effort. You aren't likely to experience the same sense of motivation and control that you do in solitary activities, so you are actually going to have to make sure that you bring some energy and enthusiasm to contribute to the team. Working with other people can, at times, be so contrary to what motivates you that in order to succeed, you have to force yourself to approach the task from another perspective. If you approach working well with other people as a challenge that's needed to realize creative opportunity, you are far more likely to succeed in a team.

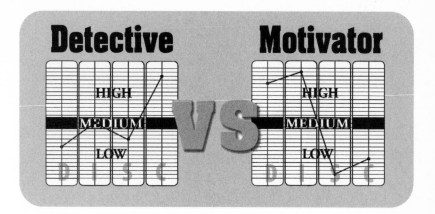

The Detective and Motivator clash over the *relative* importance of information. The Detective is known for his utter reliance on logic and reason. He focuses on the facts because accuracy is the standard by which he thinks *all* ideas should be evaluated. And why shouldn't he? The Detective's skill in gathering facts and information is unparalleled, and it serves him well in his career. The Motivator is known for being social and charming; he relies on his people skills for his sense of worth. And why shouldn't he? When the going gets tough, he's motivated by a desire to produce a satisfactory outcome for everyone involved, and people appreciate his ability to speak to the needs of different perspectives. Herein lies the problem—the Motivator follows the opinions of the group. When a team is in a tough spot, and the best way forward is uncertain, he's skilled at following the changing tide of the group's opinion. To the Motivator, it doesn't matter what the facts say; what matters is what people think. The Detective's stance in the same dilemma is the opposite; he feels the facts should decide where to go. After all, people are often wrong, and nothing blinds people to the truth more than a room full of people who hold the same opinion. Most people are quick to be swayed by this "group think," but the Detective never loses his focus on the facts.

The Detective is willing to take the time to get to the bottom of issues—no matter how obscured the facts are—and expects others to do the same. And, as much as he likes to explore information, the data on his feelings can be pretty off-limits—he isn't prone to self-disclosure. This can make the Detective come across a bit standoffish when he doesn't feel good about a Motivator's opinions. And the Motivator doesn't take kindly to naysayers. He places a strong value on being liked by others, so the Detective's resistance is quick to capture his attention.

So how do these two get to the bottom of their differences? The first thing they need to do, as with any type/anti-type pairing, is understand each other. Unlike most other personality profile conflicts, these two are unlikely to be able to talk things out. They're going to be better off establishing a quiet understanding. The skills they bring to a situation are highly unique, and don't mesh well. They both serve a distinct purpose, and their cumulative impact covers a lot of important ground in a project. This is all right, since the two don't always have to work side by side to get things done. The Motivator and Detective are better off respecting each other from a small distance. They can learn to share ideas and collaborate as the need arises. If they aren't literally hashing out problems together, the two are far more able to understand each other, and even be the target of each other's admiration. The differences in their core strengths can be fascinating to each other—as long as it's from a safe distance.

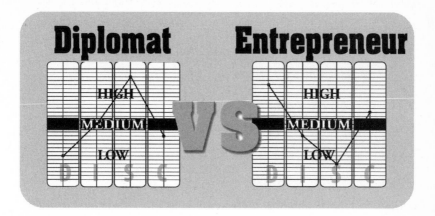

When Maude finished graduate school, she didn't have much money to call her own. Actually, once you factored in the student loans, her net worth was in the negative six figures. Despite a bevy of excellent job offers, she did what many Entrepreneurs do when they naturally follow the inclination of their personality profile—she pushed for more. She took out even more loans and started her own company, tripling the amount of her debt in less than a year. For an Entrepreneur like Maude, betraying her instinct to start this business would have meant letting an opportunity pass her by, and nothing passes Maude by—not if she has anything to say about it. Unlike the first business of many other Entrepreneurs, Maude's effort succeeded in spades, though she doesn't deserve all the credit. She owes much of her success to what, at the time, was a very humbling decision: she took on a partner.

Get close enough to Maude, and you can just about feel the ambition oozing from her pores. But ambition and instinct are rarely enough to make an Entrepreneur successful. Whether they run their own company, or work for someone else, they can never do it all on their own. Success is achieved through people. Maude realized that her tendency to push boundaries could easily run her into trouble. So she did something unusual when she started her business—she enlisted the help of a Diplomat as her partner. To Maude, it seemed that the Diplomat was someone who was everything she was not. Diplomats are great with people because they come across as humble, warm, and inviting. Diplomats focus on respect as the foundation for every relationship, working hard to ensure that people feel appreciated. These are critical qualities that employees hope for in a leader. Even running her own company, Maude had to sit back, watch, and learn from her partner.

When the two kept their motivations pointed in the same direction, they had great synergy. When they lost focus on the greater good of the company, they often clashed. Why? Because their needs were different. Maude went into business with her anti-type, an individual whose motivations and tendencies couldn't possibly be further from her own. Diplomats have little need for Dominance and control over others. Their first priority is harmony between people, and their excellent Interpersonal skills and prevailing sense of warmth are effective in creating it. A Diplomat is often the first person in a group to put the needs of others ahead of her own. When Entrepreneurs and Diplomats work together, they fit like puzzle pieces. When they clash, their needs are so unique that they confuse each other to no end. Since Diplomats work to avert conflict, they aren't quick to speak up and share what's on their mind. This makes it easy for the Entrepreneur to turn a blind eye to the problem, while the Diplomat's silent irritation grows. When you have conflict with a Diplomat, it is almost exclusively the quiet type. Though the Diplomat is uncomfortable with voicing her concerns publicly, she is open and honest about her opinions one-on-one. Entrepreneurs aren't always the best at listening, so if a Diplomat brings you her concerns, be sure to take notice and listen up—if you brush her off you may not get another chance to hear her out.

For the Diplomat, consistency is king. She works best in a comfortable, stable environment, whereas an Entrepreneur derives all of her energy from change. Diplomats don't get the same incredible rush from pushing the envelope. Likewise, the Entrepreneur feels stifled, even exhausted, in a static environment. That's why she can be so bold, even forceful, when she believes in something. She relishes feeling in control and is afraid of standing still. Entrepreneurs have to understand that most people need more time to get used to change than they do, especially a Diplomat. So, what happens when an Entrepreneur isn't able to get people on board as quickly as she'd like? She tends to work even harder, to get even more forceful, to persuade them to get behind the plan. This energy is quick to sway most people, and—though you're unlikely to hear it from the horse's mouth—Diplomats find this pushiness uncomfortable. Remember, a Diplomat needs more time to get used to new ideas than most other profiles. You can't push them into doing what you want. The Entrepreneur's flashes of instantaneous enthusiasm take Diplomats by surprise. And Diplomats don't like surprises.

An Entrepreneur is rarely going to be deeply satisfied with her accomplishments. It's not that she is some sort of tortured soul; it's just that she derives no energy from standing still. Being completely content with what she's done would turn life into a bore. Entrepreneurs spend little time basking in the glow of their accomplishments. They'd much rather move on to the next challenge. Entrepreneurs have to rack up points each day to feel successful. Be aware of this, as you're likely to find her keeping track.

Maude doesn't always take her Diplomat business partner's advice, but whenever she needs it she'll get a levelheaded perspective on the situation. And it has helped Maude sidestep some major catastrophes. As a boundary pusher, Maude is the type to always be thinking about what lies over the horizon, what's on the other side of the fence—and if putting dad's stereo on full blast can really shatter glass. It's not that she's devious for deceit's sake, but, rather, her energy and motivation are derived from taking things to a new, and often better, place. True, this boundary-pushing can lead to trouble, but when it's tempered by a Diplomat's reason it's the kind of thinking that solves intractable problems, improves the way things get done, or just plain takes people to new heights. In spite of the great potential for conflict, pairing a Diplomat and Entrepreneur together is a great idea. If they seek to understand each other and honor the other's motivations, their efforts can cover bases that neither one would ever touch on her own.

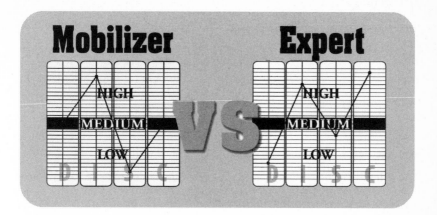

The differences between the Mobilizer and Expert profiles are unlikely to produce conflicts as fierce as those seen in the other type/anti-type pairings. The reason? These two are generally flexible, extroverted, and easygoing. They're highly social. Plus, they don't have a strong need for control, so conflict seems to slide right off them. Wow, that makes them sound like a pretty fun pair to work with. So, where's the problem that makes for a type/anti-type? The short answer is trust. The Mobilizer trusts people to a fault. She's confident in her abilities and doesn't see other people any differently. The Expert, on the other hand, is her own toughest critic. She's always looking to improve, and is hard on herself whenever she makes a mistake. Though she doesn't always admit it, she holds other people to the same high standard. This makes trust a challenge for the Expert, and people want to be trusted—showing even a shred of doubt if someone ruffles their feathers. Especially the Mobilizer, who sees no reason to doubt people.

At work, trust is the essence of delegation. Nobody likes to fail, and it's frightening to put your faith in someone who you feel is unlikely to complete the task. The Mobilizer trusts people so much that she delegates well—sometimes too well. She believes in her core that people can get the job done, and she's willing to give them a chance again and again. For her it's the ultimate sign of disrespect when an Expert isn't willing to return the favor and delegate to her. Delegating creates anxiety for the Expert because it feels like she's opening the door to failure. It's not that the Expert doubts other people more than herself; she just feels more in control when she keeps the task under her thumb. The Mobilizer is unlikely to see this as the Expert's fear of failure, but, rather, she sees it as a lack of faith in the ability of the person to whom a task has been delegated.

But Mobilizers also get stung by delegating too much. Imagine what this looks like for an Expert—watching the Mobilizer get burned by delegating just bolsters the Expert's confidence in keeping tasks to herself. If she and a Mobilizer ever lock horns over the issue of delegation, she'll likely rub this in a bit. And occasionally, the Expert's resistance to delegation is warranted, but failure to understand the motivations of her anti-type is not. From the Mobilizer's side of things, she should ensure that she's ready to listen when the Expert is ready to get honest about delegating. As outgoing and social as the Mobilizer can be, *really* listening to people is not her biggest strength. And admitting weakness is not the Expert's. Until she speaks up about her own weakness with delegating, and the Mobilizer is ready to listen, the two will continue to have a conflict in the making.

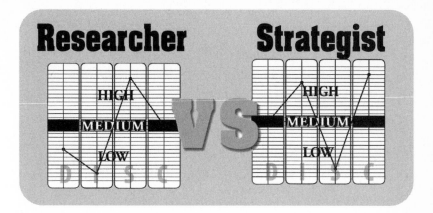

Researcher **Strategist**

What do you get when you bring two people together who are steadfast in their beliefs and always have a clear plan for the future? Unless their plans are matching, you're bound to get fireworks. Since the Researcher and Strategist are motivated by different things— yet always have a plan for the future—their opinions of where to head are often at odds. The Researcher is characterized by his outright reliance on logic and reason when solving problems. He's far more focused on tasks than people, and is understandably unresponsive to persuasive displays of emotion. If you want to convince the Researcher of something, you better come with data. The Strategist, on the other hand, is interested primarily in people, and she uses her charisma to win people over to her way of thinking. Nobody likes talking to a brick wall, which is precisely what it feels like for a Strategist to talk to a Researcher—his most persuasive arguments go unnoticed. On the other side of the coin, the Researcher doesn't understand why the Strategist can't bring the facts forward, and is quick to assume that he's hiding something to focus so fervently on, "anything other than the truth."

Task-focused profiles often clash with people-focused profiles, and the source of resolution is generally fueled by the people-focused profile's desire for harmony. This doesn't work here. The Strategist may be focused on people, but he is quick to disdain those that don't share enthusiasm for his ideas—and if anyone isn't going to, it's usually a Researcher wondering when he's going to get the facts. Since both profiles are steadfast in their beliefs about how to get things done, the butting of heads that ensues can be fierce.

Is there anything the Researcher and Strategist can do to reconcile? Absolutely. It's all about pace. You see, the Strategist is so willing to trust his gut that he grows impatient when others don't do the same. But a Researcher isn't going to budge here. Researchers just don't offer quick decisions, and the Strategist has to understand that the Researcher needs time to collect the facts before he is comfortable offering an opinion. Whenever two people have trouble staying in sync, they need to check in with each other. Since the Strategist is usually going to be the one pushing to move things forward, he needs to stop and check in with the Researcher every time that surge of impatience balloons in his belly. Make sure the two of you are talking about the same thing. The Researcher won't hesitate to tell you the crux of what he's thinking—so take what he says seriously.

If you think emotions can't be measured, watch how quickly people are swayed by the Strategist's ideas. He's no Pied Piper—he's convincing because he speaks directly to what people feel is important. The Strategist is also very good at planning ahead. He's so good at it that people place great trust in what he thinks. So you're better off paying attention to what's on his mind. If you're hesitant to consider his suggestions, make sure it's truly a logical fallacy and not your own resistance to change. The Strategist embraces change like a warm hug, and a Researcher can learn a lot from that. Finally, realize that the Strategist's use of emotion to sway people's opinion distracts from an important quality that he shares with the Researcher—perhaps more than any other types, the Strategist and the Researcher like to dot the i's and cross the t's. When things are going to hell in a handbasket, the Strategist is not only going to care about doing things right, he can convince the group to listen to a Researcher's reason. Like the Researcher, the Strategist is a smart, logical thinker; when they find common ground in support of a plan, they make a formidable team.

Epilogue: Moving Forward

I NEVER HAD the chance to meet William Marston, the creator of the DISC, who died in 1947, before I was born. But a few years back, I was lucky enough to come across someone who did. I met Dorothy in San Diego at an emotional intelligence certification workshop held by my company. She was a woman in the twilight of her career, working as an independent consultant to companies that needed help designing and delivering employee training programs. When the discussion in the room turned to self-awareness, she shared her experience meeting William Marston, and cited it as a powerful influence upon her career in training. Dorothy was just a teen when she met him. At the time, she was volunteering as a candy striper in a local hospital, and Marston spent his last days on earth on her floor. Back then, comic books were a new and intensely popular form of entertainment for people her age, and Marston was a larger-than-life figure because he created the Wonder Woman character. Marston conjured up Wonder Woman as an empowering role model for young women, housed in a medium that adolescents would surely read—comic books. As Marston reflected on his life, their conversation turned from comic books to personality, and he explained his DISC model to her. Marston shared just one regret that day from his hospital bed, and it's stuck with Dorothy to this day. He told her that the fame that came from his work with Wonder Woman pulled him away from further study of personality. He knew there was more work to be done in understanding personality, and he longed to see what would develop. His only regret in death was that he wouldn't get to see what happened next.

I like to think that this book helps Marston to realize this vision; that it continues to unlock the mysteries inherent in our personality code. Marston lived in a time when the mind was still an enigma, yet he saw things that no one else could. Today we have the unprecedented opportunity to understand how the mind works—including the physical basis for thought inside the brain. Modern neuroscience confirms what Marston suggested more than seven decades ago: our strengths, motivations, and tendencies are dictated by fixed elements of our character—the personality. By the time we reach adulthood, personality is hardwired in the brain. It serves as the conduit by which our minds act—the mental funnel through which our choices must flow. Marston's DISC model has withstood the scrutiny of experimental evaluation, and it has grown beyond the four character traits to reveal fourteen unique types of people. In the TalentSmart study, we witnessed how understanding your personality type breeds success. People who harness this unique brand of self-awareness are remarkably clear about their capabilities and capacities; they know the situations and people that can help make them successful.

Common "wisdom" used to suggest that we make ourselves into the person we wish to become. Today we know better than this. Success comes in knowing who you are—in applying your natural strengths to reach your goals. In the end, we move forward guided by the answers inherent in our personality code. Dr. Marston wouldn't have wanted it any other way.

Appendix A. Inside the IDISC

The following Q&A was prepared by the TalentSmart team of Tanya Goodwin-Maslach, Alexandria Herrera, Jean H. Riley, Nicholas Tasler, and Lac D. Su.

PSYCHOLOGICAL TESTS are often shrouded in mystery, but they don't have to be. The principles by which they operate are straightforward enough to be understood by anyone who wishes to explore them. This is the primary goal of this section. It will help you to understand how the IDISC works and lift the curtain to reveal how the IDISC measures human personality.

What is the IDISC?

The IDISC is a test that quickly and accurately measures your personality profile. Personality is the often misunderstood term used to describe people's preferences and tendencies for interacting with the world around them. Like the tendency toward introversion or extraversion, these traits influence how we think, how we feel, and ultimately what we do. Each of us has a personality profile that reflects our own unique blend of the personality traits, and is produced by hardwired paths for thinking in the brain. By the time we reach adulthood, these paths are fixed. They serve as the conduits by which our brains think, the mental funnels through which our choices must flow. Personality is a collection of our motivations, needs, and preferences that serves as a blueprint to our strengths and weaknesses—each individual's "code," as it were.

For the past two thousand years, the study of human behavior has pointed to four dimensions of personality in the individual. The varying presence of all four dimensions in each of us creates a unique personality profile. In the last century, standardization and rigor in psychological science provided names for, definitions, and accurate measurement of these dimensions. The four dimensions measured by the IDISC are Dominant, Interpersonal, Steady, and Conscientious. The IDISC follows up with easy-to-understand recommendations that are customized to fit the user's unique personality profile. Though the calculations used to produce the IDISC scores are rather complicated, the feedback the test provides is generally easy to understand. Rather than a confusing batch of numbers with no relevant anchor in the world around you, the IDISC provides feedback in terms you already use. The test results reveal the degree to which you display each of the DISC personality traits, as well as your overall personality type—a combination of these four unique traits. There are fourteen DISC personality types, and the IDISC reveals which of the fourteen best applies to you.

A single use of the IDISC is complimentary with the purchase of this book, via a unique passcode printed on the inside of the book's jacket. Your test code may be used only once, but your results never expire. You can return to www.personalitycode.com at any time to log on to the system, use the interactive e-learning, set goals in the goal tracking system, and learn from the dynamic action plans that are incorporated into your feedback report. Otherwise, the test is available separately from Talent Smart.com. The average time to complete the IDISC online is about fifteen minutes.

On what theory of personality is the IDISC based?

William Moulton Marston, Ph.D. (1893–1947), is credited with creating the DISC model, which he introduced in his 1928 book *Emotions of Normal People,* in which he described people as behaving along two axes. The first axis captures how individuals respond to their environment, whether they are active or reactive. The second axis, originally labeled "antagonistic and favorable," depends on people's perception of their environment; now more appropriately labeled "task-oriented and people-oriented." When placed as right angles, the two axes form four quadrants that explain four behavioral patterns.

- **Dominant** describes those who are active and task-oriented. They are assertive and prefer power and control.
- **Interpersonal** (Inducement or Influence) depicts those who are active and people-oriented. They enjoy social situations and rely on their communication skills.
- **Steady** portrays individuals who are reactive and task-oriented. They are thoughtful people who are patient and persistent.
- **Conscientious** (Compliance or Cautious) represents individuals who are reactive and people-oriented. They seek organization and structure.

Marston originally sought to understand how normal human emotions led individuals to behave in reaction to their environment. He developed the DISC model to help individuals gain a better understanding of not only their behavior, but the behaviors of others. Since then, the DISC model has evolved continuously into a comprehensive tool that measures the intensity of the four factors and combines how they interact with one another, allowing an individual to identify her personality profile.

Why is the TalentSmart IDISC Personality Profile based on William Marston's model of personality and not another?

First, the Marston model of personality is the longest-standing and most widely utilized. Marston's DISC dimensions of behavior have withstood more than seventy years of scrutiny, evaluation, and modification. Second, we've found that Marston's DISC model is the most intuitive model of personality. People find it easy to understand and use, and this likely accounts for its longevity. Third, when you consider other prevailing methods of measuring personality, most have limited, questionable, or no scientific research to support their validity.

Is the TalentSmart IDISC personality profiler identical to Marston's original DISC model?

The fourteen personality profiles in the IDISC come from a decade of research that yielded a modernized interpretation of Marston's DISC model. Marston's original model never moved beyond the D, I, S, and C facets of our character. The IDISC considers these four components, as well as the combination of these four traits in any individual, to yield a personality type—of which there are fourteen possible.

Why are there fourteen personality types?

The fourteen IDISC personality types are each a unique combination of the four DISC personality traits (Dominant, Interpersonal, Steady, and Conscientious). Through an extended series of statistical analyses, we were able to factor-analyze and condense the 123,000 possible personality configurations into fourteen unique personality types. Each of these fourteen personality types are statistically distinct from one another—they don't have significant overlap with another type, and they represent the fourteen kinds of people that can be readily discerned based upon their fixed personalities.

How prevalent are
the fourteen IDISC personality types?

The following percentages represent the prevalence of each type in the general population:

The Ally—5% of the population

The Architect—13% of the population

The Coach—9% of the population

The Detective—9% of the population

The Diplomat—9% of the population

The Entrepreneur—7% of the population

The Expert—6% of the population

The Innovator—3% of the population

The Mobilizer—3% of the population

The Motivator—13% of the population

The Opportunist—2% of the population

The Researcher—4% of the population

The Sponsor—16% of the population

The Strategist—1% of the population

Is it possible to have more than one personality type?

Personality traits are generally regarded as being stable and enduring throughout the course of a person's adult life. For practical purposes, we can be certain that the typical person's personality will not change enough to make appreciable differences over the course of a lifetime. For example, through diligent practice a person can learn to pay more attention to a specific trait, such as attention to detail. A conscious effort to pay more attention to details over the course of years may appear to improve your Conscientiousness (one of the four personality traits). However, consciously raising your awareness to details does not make you a *naturally* "detail-oriented" person. It simply increases how often you consciously choose to exhibit one of the many behavioral facets that combine to form the Conscientious dimension of personality. It doesn't change enough to make a difference.

Why should I learn my personality profile if I can't change it?

The TalentSmart study shows that self-awareness is the key to success personally and professionally. Learning your personality profile is the single greatest task in which you can engage to increase your self-awareness. Your profile reveals the essence of your motivations, tendencies, and preferences. Every day, whether you are aware of it or not, your personality drives your actions in many ways. When you discover your profile, you also have a window to the people, situations, and tasks that will help you to get what you want from life. You can use this knowledge to eliminate obstacles in your path and accelerate your success.

Can you learn to spot someone's personality profile without the test?

Absolutely. It isn't very easy to pinpoint the specific profile someone has, but it is quite possible. Once you've spent some time learning the DISC model (about the time you've finished this book and studied your profile online), you'll discover that it's pretty easy to spot whether people you know have the prevailing tendency to be Dominant, Interpersonal, Steady, or Conscientious. The fourteen personality types can be clustered along these dimensions.

The fourteen DISC types according to their prevailing tendency to be Dominant, Interpersonal, Steady, or Conscientious. If you remember that each type tends to favor one of the four DISC traits, it's easy to see how they cluster and easy to understand people on the basis of the prevailing quality of their personality.

For whom was the IDISC designed?

The IDISC is a distinct departure from the typical psychological test because it is designed for the individual seeking to learn more about his or her personality. The test results come in an easy-to-read format that is simple to download and print out. The results are so easy to follow that anyone can use the IDISC without the help of interpretation from a psychologist or coach. The IDISC does not require prerequisite educational degrees, credentials, or certification to use. It is fairly common for personality tests to require such background to understand the complicated feedback they provide. The user-friendly format of the IDISC ensures that anyone can use it to his or her advantage.

Is the IDISC designed for use at work or at home?

Personality is a stable collection of the tendencies, strengths, motivations, and preferences that follow us wherever we go. Therefore, you can use the IDISC in whatever setting you like—your score will not change. Your personality profile is so predominant and stable that you can think of all aspects of your life when you answer the questions. Your results will be the same, and will be useful to apply in most settings. However, be careful when answering the questions. You should answer according to who you *really* are, rather than the person you want to be. Be honest with the IDISC and it will be honest with you. Most people don't have to think too hard on this one; just answer the questions according to what you tend to say and do on a daily basis.

Should the IDISC be used for employee selection?

TalentSmart does not promote, recommend, or support the use of the IDISC for hiring or employee selection purposes. Any test that hasn't been validated inside your organization shouldn't be used in hiring and selection. The IDISC is a training and development tool that should be used to heighten an individual's awareness of their behavior. If you use the test for selection purposes, it may expose your company to Equal Employment Opportunity Commission (EEOC) claims for adverse impact or potential discriminatory effect on applicants. This is not intended to be legal advice, and the author suggests you seek the advice of a qualified legal professional.

Is the information I enter secure?

Yes. All responses to the IDISC are stored on a secure, remote server, and your scores are held in the strictest confidence. The server has dedicated bandwidth that ensures that hundreds of thousands of people can access the system at the same time without any reduction in the speed of the application or the quality of its function. Since your information is password protected, you are the only one who can access your test scores, saved comments, or goals set in the goal-tracking system.

Does my IDISC personality profile expire?

The free passcode that comes with the purchase of this book does not expire, and you can use it anytime. Once you take your IDISC, you will have immediate access to your results and e-learning and can come back and see them online anytime you wish. You can view your customized feedback report online or you can download it in PDF format to save on your computer. This feature allows you the freedom to use the feedback report at your convenience. If you take the complimentary test provided by this book, simply go back to www.personalitycode.com, enter your e-mail and password, and click "Log In" to view your report. If you've forgotten your user name and password, the unique survey code printed on the reverse side of the book's jacket will also give you access to your results after you've taken the test.

Why is the e-learning included?

E-learning was added to the IDISC feedback because the authors felt that simply delivering a profile was not enough information to really help someone understand personality and leverage his or her strengths. E-learning is intended to move the experience beyond taking a test, and, instead, make it an engaging interactive learning experience. The Web-based IDISC tabulates your scores automatically and links your results to online activities that illustrate personality in action. This e-learning is customized to your unique personality profile, and it lets you work at your own pace. You can also print out the report, save it on your computer, and even share it with friends, colleagues, and family if you wish.

The goal-tracking system allows you to set goals based upon your personality profile, and share these goals—and your profile—with other people. This process will support your ability to leverage your personality to achieve positive results. This can be accomplished by choosing from the sample goals provided in the system, or setting some of your own unique goals, and indicating who to share them with. If you want electronic reminders to chart your progress and update the goals you've set, the system will provide them for you automatically. The IDISC report provides your personality's strengths, challenges, defining characteristics, how to make the most of your profile, and suggestions for how others can work with you. It provides practical recommendations for leveraging your personality profile, and action plans to help you harness your unique talents and strengths.

What do the video clips accomplish?

The e-learning included in the IDISC feedback incorporates short film clips that illustrate each of the personality types in action. The video clips are a tool to keep you engaged in what you're learning, and they illustrate key points about your IDISC personality profile. Video clips help you to discover and interpret the nuances of personality in the actions of others, as well as raise your own self-awareness.

Is the IDISC available in other languages?

The IDISC will be released in other languages along with the foreign editions of this book. Check www.personalitycode.com for information on upcoming non-English editions of the book.

How was the IDISC designed?

The test was designed and developed by a team of researchers holding advanced degrees in behavioral science. Test items were pooled conceptually, analyzed, and modified or removed in an iterative process to ensure that each captured one of the four components of Marston's DISC model. During the course of the TalentSmart study, a broad pool of 346 test questions accumulated that measured personality and related behavioral traits. The final version of the test only utilized the statements that were *necessary* and *sufficient* to measure the core of the DISC model. The term *necessary* refers to all questions that were required to ensure that a component of the DISC model was adequately represented. The term *sufficient* refers to eliminating unnecessary items that would otherwise produce redundancy. In other words, no extra questions were added to the test, and no items that were required went missing. Statisticians oversaw every step of this process, and the specific techniques utilized are described in detail in later questions of this appendix.

Tests of face validity ensured that those taking the test would perceive the test questions (also known as "items") as intuitive and straightforward representations of Marston's DISC model. The IDISC uses a positive approach, ensuring that adjectives used to describe the person taking the test are perceived to be on the "same level" in the eyes of that individual. This ensures that any question has a similar likelihood of being chosen by any single user, as the relative positive or negative connotation of the items is equal. This, by nature, reduces the tendency to avoid items that would make the respondent appear negatively, and increases the reliability and validity of the test. The pool of items that met these criteria went through a statistically iterative process, to remove those items that did not contribute to the validity of the component of the DISC model being measured. The resulting length of the test represents the number of statement quartets (groups of four adjectives that participants must choose from) that is both necessary and sufficient to capture the core of your DISC personality profile.

How was the IDISC normed?

Norms are descriptive standards against which individuals can compare their performance to the performance of other people. In other words, a score on a self-report test means little in and of itself. The value or meaning of the score is derived from what it is compared to—or based on—and is derived from the parameters of the possible scores that can be obtained. The IDISC compares each individual's responses against a large normative database of more than 100,000 responses, to ensure an objective comparison of his or her personality. The normative sample includes male and female subjects, ages eighteen to eighty-plus years, working in virtually every industry and virtually every job function worldwide. These responses were collected from English speakers on six continents.

Does the IDISC reduce self-serving bias?

At some level, we all want to look good and inflate our scores. Self-serving bias is our tendency to enhance self-scoring assessments, taking credit for our successes (the self-enhancing bias) and denying any responsibility for failure (the self-protective bias). Although it is almost impossible to completely eliminate self-serving bias in self-report tests, the issue of self-serving bias is less relevant for the IDISC than most self assessments because it measures your tendency to exhibit unique behaviors without preference of one behavior over another. The IDISC uses proprietary surveying methods that balance the effect of self-serving responses where they occur. You can consciously fake a score profile by choosing random answers that you know don't apply to you, but you can only do this intentionally. Otherwise the test will correct your scores to provide an accurate measure of your personality profile.

Why does the IDISC use the 112 adjectives that are in the questions and not others? Why are these adjectives paired into twenty-eight groups of four?

The 112 adjectives in the test are designed to eliminate the biases that are common with an individual's self-perception. The adjectives are neutrally weighted to ensure that people are unlikely to prefer one of these descriptors over another. This ensures that people answer honestly about what they tend to say and do rather than what they wish was a description of their behavior. For more on how the list of adjectives used in the test was culled to a manageable and statistically valid final list, see "Is the IDISC scientifically valid?" on page 159. The adjectives are paired into twenty-eight groups of four to create a forced choice, where you must choose the one adjective that *best* describes your behavior and the one that *least* describes your behavior. Each of the adjectives corresponds to one aspect of the DISC model, and they are randomized in their presentation to test users. A participant completing the IDISC unwittingly outlines the nature of her personality through the items that are chosen or rejected. The 112 adjectives used in the IDISC are listed in the table that follows.

The 112 Personality Trait Adjectives of the IDISC Personality Profiler

Accommodating	Carefree	Cooperative
Active	Careful	Cordial
Adventurous	Casual	Dependable
Agreeable	Charismatic	Diplomatic
Analytical	Cheerful	Disciplined
Animated	Communicative	Discreet
Approachable	Competitive	Domineering
Assertive	Complimentary	Driven
Attentive	Conforming	Eager
Authoritative	Conscientious	Effective
Balanced	Conservative	Enthusiastic
Bold	Considerate	Exacting
Brazen	Consistent	Excited
Candid	Content	Extroverted
Captivating	Coolheaded	Fair

Faithful	Laid-back	Reserved
Fearless	Lively	Resilient
Firm	Low-key	Respectful
Flexible	Magnetic	Responsible
Focused	Mellow	Self-confident
Forgiving	Observant	Sharp
Forward	Outgoing	Social
Fun-loving	Painstaking	Spirited
Giving	Particular	Stable
Good-natured	Passionate	Steady
Gracious	Patient	Structured
Hopeful	Perceptive	Sympathetic
Hospitable	Persistent	Talkative
Humble	Persuasive	Thoughtful
Impartial	Pleasant	Traditional
Independent	Polite	Trustworthy
Influential	Positive	Understanding
Innovative	Precise	Unwavering
Inspiring	Private	Upbeat
Instinctive	Quirky	Warm
Intuitive	Rational	Willful
Inventive	Rebellious	
Jovial	Reliable	

Is the IDISC scientifically valid?

The psychometric strength of the IDISC embodies the years of research and empirical evaluation that went into its development. The reliability and validity of the test are continually monitored as new data accumulates to ensure that the test remains an accurate measurement of your personality profile. How do you know a test does a good job of measuring the concept it purports to measure? First, it's critical that any test follows the well-established design and validation standards set forth by the American Psychological Association, and the IDISC exceeds these standards.

Reliability is a term used to describe the tendency for clusters of items to consistently measure an associated construct. That is, a reliable assessment measures a concept consistently, but this doesn't mean it's measuring what it's supposed to be measuring. For example, while there are many reliable tests, relatively few of them predict important life outcomes. Each of the four components of the DISC model within the IDISC assessment generates a reliability score, which is measured using the Cronbach's alpha statistic. Cronbach's alpha ranges from 0.0 to 1.0. The values for the four reliability scores of the components of the IDISC range from .76 to .80, which is considered to be a strong indication that the test is reliable. The standard level of acceptable reliability for the Cronbach's alpha statistic is .70 to .95. Values lower than .70 suggest an improper internal reliability, or that the questions don't really belong together. Values above .95 suggest the items aren't really unique. For example, if I write the test question "Are you intelligent?" followed by "Are you smart?" the reliability of these questions together would almost certainly fall above .95, because they are measuring the same thing. The table on page 161 indexes the IDISC reliability coefficients.

To determine a test's ability to measure real-world outcomes, you turn to psychometric validity. A valid measure is one that captures the concept it was designed to measure. In order to be valid, an assessment needs to be deemed reliable, but a reliable assessment isn't necessarily a

IDISC Factors	Reliability Coefficients
Dominant	.79
Interpersonal	.80
Steady	.76
Conscientious	.76

valid one. There are many ways to measure validity, including comparison to a criterion of interest, such as job performance. Since no one IDISC personality profile is better than any other, there is no direct relationship between the test and job performance. It's true that certain profiles will help with specific elements of some jobs (aka the Motivator as a salesman), but these relationships are not broad enough to infer significant conclusions. For the DISC model, the essential measure of a test's validity is the extent to which the model is accurately represented through interscale correlations. In the DISC model, Dominant and Steady are dimensions consistently found to be near opposites, as are the Interpersonal and Conscientious dimensions. The statistic used for this analysis is the correlation coefficient, a measure that indicates the strength and direction of a linear relationship between two variables. If that number is positive, the variables have a positive relationship—that is, they go up and down together. If the correlation coefficient is negative, the opposite occurs. The correlation coefficient, like the Cronbach's alpha, is measured on a scale from 0.0 to 1.0. The most established method for calculating a correlation is the Pearson product-moment. The Pearson product-moment correlation coefficient is calculated by dividing the covariance of two variables by their standard deviations. The higher the value of the correlation coefficient, the stronger the relationship between the variables, and the less they are likely to be independent. As expected, in the IDISC these dimensions are negatively correlated, or are near opposites. The following table shows the interscale correlations for the four dimensions of the IDISC.

	D-Most	I-Most	S-Most	C-Most	D-Least	I-Least	S-Least	C-Least
Reliability Coefficients and Interscale Correlations Among Most and Least Scores								
D-Most	.68							
I-Most	-.13	.76						
S-Most	-.62	-.34	.66					
C-Most	-.16	-.72	.03	.71				
D-Least	-.69	-.05	.57	.17	.73			
I-Least	.06	-.69	.18	.61	-.09	.71		
S-Least	.61	.14	-.66	-.09	-.67	-.20	.69	
C-Least	.17	.61	-.19	-.69	-.34	-.61	.06	.68

Reliability coefficients are shown in bold along the diagonal of the table. Interscale correlations are shown below the diagonal.

How can the IDISC be accurate with only twenty-eight questions?

Contrary to common belief, profile testing does not require large numbers of questions in order to accurately measure your personality. Psychological tests simply don't require this length to be reliable and valid. True, it is more difficult to create a shorter test that retains the characteristics of validity and reliability, but that's why TalentSmart spends years developing a new assessment before releasing it. The tradition of lengthy tests in the form of questionnaires often has more to do with the subject feeling like they have been accurately assessed than the validity of the questionnaire. It's more common to find a test that is too long than one that is too short, because many of the test items add little to the power of the assessment. An excellent example of a good assessment—one that is short yet scientifically valid—is the Beck Depression Inventory (BDI). The BDI is the most trusted measure of depression available; it is used by health-care providers worldwide. The BDI measures depression (a single construct) with just thirteen questions. The IDISC works similarly in measuring the four dimensions of personality with twenty-eight questions.

Appendix B: Behind the Scenes of the TalentSmart Study

NUMBERS ARE powerful. Lest we dare forget, we often receive reminders in the letters and e-mails that come from people whose lives have been altered by the numbers in our research. One letter that will always be near to our hearts came earlier this year from a women's correctional facility in Oregon. Facility staff created and delivered a self-awareness training program for the inmates based on our first book, *The Emotional Intelligence Quick Book,* and we received a letter from an attendee that began, "If I had learned what your book taught me sooner, I wouldn't be stuck inside these walls today." It's our business to discover what qualities propel successful people—both individually and collectively as an organization—so that anyone can apply these skills to his or her benefit. Numbers may be powerful, but they only tell half the story. In the end, they are only as powerful as the lives they touch.

Our journey began in the mid-1990s, when we grappled with the question "Is there a quality that any person can use to his or her benefit to be more successful in life?" The TalentSmart study is an ongoing search for the answer to this question. In Chapter 2, you learned the relatively short answer—self-awareness. Here you'll follow us through the process by which we "stumbled" upon this answer.

Step 1. Sizing Up the Whole Person

People's thoughts, actions, and words are the product of three unique mental capacities—intelligence (IQ), emotional intelligence (EQ), and personality. Though we can't predict one on the basis of the other, we can measure them collectively in any person. Intelligence is the least flexible of the three. Your IQ, short of a traumatic event like a brain injury, is fixed from a very young age. Intelligence isn't what you know, but the ability to acquire facts and information. IQ is measured in comparison to your peers, and most people are nearly identical at age fifteen as they are at age fifty. Intelligence is—for obvious reasons—important to success. Scientists began measuring IQ in the early 1900s, and they realized that it was a fast method to separate superior performers from those who were subpar. But they were quick to notice that IQ lacked something important. Many people were incredibly intelligent but limited by their ability to manage their behavior and get along well with others. There were also people who excelled in life despite having average intelligence. The study of IQ has continued through the decades, but has gleaned little significant new information that benefits the study of personal excellence. People are as smart as they are going to be at a very young age, and measuring their intelligence does little to help them improve. Since IQ captures but a small portion of the whole picture of any single person's intelligence, it wasn't measured in the TalentSmart study.

The mental capacities that IQ researchers have seen playing an important role beyond IQ are emotional intelligence (EQ) and personality. Emotional intelligence skills are soft skills—they are flexible and readily learned. While it is true that some people are naturally more emotionally intelligent than others, a high EQ can be developed even if you aren't born with it. The discovery of EQ gave researchers worldwide a new name for the skill that explains why two people of the same intelligence can attain vastly different levels of success in life. Emotional intelligence taps into a fundamental element of human behavior that is unique from your intellect. There is no known connection between IQ and EQ; you simply can't predict emotional intelligence on the basis of how smart someone is. Emotional intelligence is your ability to recognize and

SIZING UP THE WHOLE PERSON

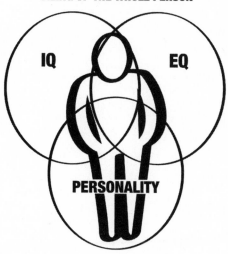

Intelligence (IQ), personality, and emotional intelligence (EQ) are distinct qualities we all possess. Together they determine how we think and act, and it is impossible to predict one based upon the other. Of the three, emotional intelligence is the only quality that is flexible and able to change.

understand emotions, and your skill at using this awareness to manage yourself and relationships with others. There is one nutshell description we like to share to keep things simple: "Emotional intelligence describes the side of life that typical smarts cannot." We measured EQ using a twenty-eight-question test called The Emotional Intelligence Appraisal. The Emotional Intelligence Appraisal measures what are largely considered to be the four prevailing emotional intelligence skills in the areas of personal and social competence: self-awareness, self-management, social awareness, and relationship management. We describe these as "soft skills" because they can change readily over the course of a lifetime. One can increase or decrease EQ with effort, and it tends to grow and shrink in response to the changing circumstances life throws our way.

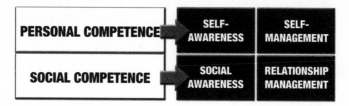

The Four Emotional Intelligence (EQ) Soft Skills

PERSONAL COMPETENCE	SELF-AWARENESS	SELF-MANAGEMENT
SOCIAL COMPETENCE	SOCIAL AWARENESS	RELATIONSHIP MANAGEMENT

Self-Awareness: The ability to accurately perceive your own emotions in the moment and understand your tendencies across situations. Self-awareness includes keeping on top of your typical reaction to specific events, challenges, and even people. A high degree of self-awareness requires a willingness to tolerate the discomfort of knowing what your weaknesses are—in addition to your strengths.

Self-Management: The ability to use awareness of your emotions to stay flexible and positively direct your behavior. This means managing your emotional reactions to situations and people.

Social Awareness: The ability to accurately pick up on emotions in other people and understand what is really going on with them. This often means perceiving what other people are thinking and feeling even if you do not feel the same way.

Relationship Management: The ability to use awareness of your own emotions and the emotions of others to manage interactions successfully. This ensures clear communication and effective handling of conflict.

Many theorists find value in breaking down soft skills into additional components beyond the four emotional intelligence skills. For this reason, we explored hundreds of articles on soft skills and found an additional twenty-two skills to measure in addition to emotional intelligence (see box, "The 'Other' Soft Skills of the TalentSmart Study" on pages 171–173). We crafted an additional 127 test questions to measure these twenty-two skills, and, together with the twenty-eight emotional intelligence questions, the entire battery of soft skills in the TalentSmart study contained 155 test questions. These questions were written as *behavioral impact statements,* a proprietary method of creating assessments that are brief and highly accurate. The behavioral impact method enables an assessment to measure a broader range of skills in a shorter period of time, increasing the accuracy of a subject's responding by both taking the focus away from responses that are *right* or *wrong* and by keeping their attention while they are taking the test. For example, the competency titled "communication" does not ask questions about every specific method of communication that a manager may use in the workplace. Rather, it assesses the impact of a manager's ability to communicate by measuring coworkers' reactions to the manager's communicative behaviors.

The authors used an iterative process of writing draft questions and reworking them to fit what is *necessary* and *sufficient* (no more and no less than what covers the elements of that skill) to assess each competency. This proprietary model of drafting survey questions eliminates unnecessary questions by avoiding the practice of using many specific behavioral questions to measure a single skill. Instead, the test questions measure the sufficient behavioral outcome needed to adequately assess a particular skill. The survey questions used in the assessments describe critical aspects of each of the twenty-six skills through the typical behavior of the individual being assessed. The frequency with which an individual demonstrates behaviors related to a skill are the best measure of that skill. Therefore, the test questions are structured using a six-point frequency scale, which narrows in on the frequency with which the individual demonstrates the particular behavior in question. A sample test question looks something like this:

How often are you confident in your abilities?

Select the single option that best applies to you.

___ NEVER   ___ USUALLY

___ RARELY   ___ ALMOST ALWAYS

___ SOMETIMES   ___ ALWAYS

The "Other" Soft Skills of the TalentSmart Study

Risk-Taking: The ability to maneuver through situations that require risk and stand behind your actions long enough to see them through when the going gets tough.

Planning: Anticipate upcoming events in order to set appropriate goals and get things done.

Vision: Inspired people take others in new directions. This requires the ability to envision a new reality for others that they can see and want to pursue.

Courage: Standing strong in the face of adversity.

Decision-making: Making sound decisions that consider multiple options, seek input from others when appropriate, and are reached in a timely manner.

Communication: The act of expressing information clearly to others verbally and in writing.

Acumen: Active curiosity about the world around you that translates into striving to learn.

Mobilizing Others: The ability to motivate and influence those around you.

Research: The skill of discovering what pieces of information really matter to make a good decision.

Results-Focus: Keeping your "eyes on the prize." They focus on the end result and do what it takes to get there.

Information-Sharing: Once decisions have been made, the act of sharing how the decision was reached with those whom it affects.

Rehearsal: How well you train your instincts in your decision-making. It's about practicing using your rules over and over again until they become habit.

Outcome Concern: The act of being genuinely concerned with the welfare of others and expressing this concern on a personal level.

Teamwork: Placing the needs of the team before your own, and being humble enough to share in successes with the group.

Flexibility: The act of constantly adapting to your surroundings. Being able to respond quickly to uncertainty and change.

Building Commitment: Sharing the information that others need to perform. Going the extra mile to show others that you care.

Empowerment: Empowering people by involving them directly in your activities and respecting their input and perspective.

Rules: How you devise a system to guide your instincts. It is about protecting yourself from making predictable errors in judgment.

Integrity: The melding of ethics and values into action. Individuals who display this quality operate off of a core set of beliefs that gain admiration and support from others.

Credibility: Those who walk their talk and can be counted on to do what they say they are going to do.

Values Differences: Valuing the different perspectives that people bring to a situation.

Lifelong Learning: The act of constantly trying to learn about yourself to grow and become the best person you can be.

With IQ excluded on the basis of prior research findings, and twenty-six soft skills measured via 155 survey questions, personality was the final piece of the puzzle. Personality is the stable "style" that defines each of us, and has been described in detail in this book. Personality is unique from soft skills because it's inflexible; it's composed of stable traits that capture the essence of your character. You can't predict an individual's personality on the basis of her IQ or EQ. Also, personality can't be used to predict job performance and life satisfaction—we saw high and low levels of these variables associated with every personality type. That is, which type you are says very little about what you can achieve or whether or not you'll be happy. The important thing is to fully understand your particular personality type, because the key to success is self-awareness. The remainder of this appendix considers the relationship between the twenty-six soft skills of the TalentSmart study and job performance and life satisfaction.

Step 2. Collecting the Data

The TalentSmart study database contains responses representing 500,000 participants gathered over more than a decade. Our goal was to accumulate as diverse a sample as possible, so that we could make interpretations that represent truths common to all types of people. Approximately 82% of the sample completed our tests via the Internet, and 28% completed tests on pencil and paper. The paper and pencil tests were mechanically scored and transferred into the database. Participants in the study came from three places:

1. Those recruited to take the tests via Internet advertisements and word-of-mouth referrals.
2. TalentSmart individual testing clients, who participated in the testing for career and personal development.
3. Employees of organizations who had retained our services for departmental and company-wide assessment of the employee population.

Step 3. Analyzing the Results

Prior to comparing scores on the assessment scales to outcomes, statistical analyses were used to confirm the validity of the underlying structure of the assessments. The goal here was to determine if the design of the instruments—how the items were grouped—was confirmed by the data

Demographics of the TalentSmart Study

Continents	**All six inhabited continents**
Countries	**133 countries** North America, Central America, Caribbean: 27; South America: 13; Europe: 39; Africa: 20; Asia: 31; Australia: 3
Gender	**51% male; 49% female**
Age	**18–93 years**
Occupation	**15 unique areas** Sales, marketing, finance, accounting, operations, customer service, human resources, organizational development, learning, IT/IS, engineering, business development, manufacturing/production, research and development, and unemployed
Job Title	**Seven classifications** Individual contributor, supervisor, manager, director, executive, senior executive/VP, and CEO

we collected. This first step in evaluating items in a survey concerns the concept of "face validity." Face validity pertains to whether the test questions appear to be a valid representation of the concept, so that observers and assessment examinees will accept the results. Once the survey questions met the face validity criteria, they were presented "cold" to additional subject matter experts for further confirmation. The subject matter experts used in the TalentSmart study included doctorate- and master-level psychologists, as well as MBA-trained businesspeople with executive-level experience.

The next step was to ascertain the reliability of the assessments. Reliability is a term used to describe the tendency for clusters of items to consistently measure an associated construct. Each of the twenty-six skills assessed in the TalentSmart study generates a unique reliability score, which is measured using the Cronbach's alpha statistic. Cronbach's alpha ranges from 0.0 to 1.0. The values for the reliability scores of the twenty-six competencies ranged from .67 to .95, which is considered a strong indication of the reliability of the assessments used in the

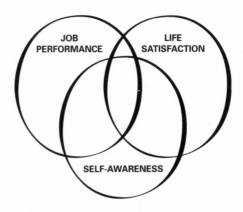

Relationship of Self-Awareness to Job Performance and Life Satisfaction.

Cronbach's Alpha Reliability Coefficients for the Assessment Competencies in the TalentSmart Study

Competency	Number of Items	Cronbach's Alpha
Self-Awareness	6	.92
Self-Management	9	.84
Social Awareness	5	.79
Relationship Management	8	.87
Risk-Taking	5	.94
Planning	4	.93
Vision	4	.90
Courage	4	.92
Decision-Making	5	.94
Communication	5	.93
Acumen	4	.88
Mobilizing Others	6	.90
Research	8	.80
Results Focus	12	.93
Information-Sharing	3	.94
Rehearsal	10	.67
Outcome Concern	3	.92
Teamwork	16	.81
Flexibility	5	.92
Building Commitment	4	.92
Empowerment	4	.95
Rules	6	.67
Integrity	5	.95
Credibility	4	.93
Values Differences	4	.92
Lifelong Learning	4	.92

study. The reliabilities measured for each of the twenty-six competencies are listed in the table on page 179.

The final, critical step compared assessment scores with important outcomes in life. By sizing up each of the twenty-six soft skills against job performance, job satisfaction, and life satisfaction, we were able to assess the incremental contribution of each skill upon the outcome, and assess the significance of the relationship between each skill and each outcome. The relative contribution of each of the twenty-six soft skills reveals how important (or not) each skill is for obtaining desired results in life. The following image illustrates the connection between a predictor variable (a soft skill, such as self-awareness) and outcome variables (in this case, life satisfaction and job performance). Overlapping circles suggest a strong connection between these variables, as there was between self-awareness and life satisfaction and job performance. We made similar comparisons for all twenty-six soft skills measured by the TalentSmart study. Multiple regression was the statistical technique used to make these comparisons. The multiple regression calculation yields a multiple regression correlation coefficient, or R-squared. R-squared is a number between zero and one. A value close to zero suggests an inability of the variable included to explain the result you've witnessed. For example, R-squared values for the twenty-six soft skill competencies were all over the map. Some skills yielded very high R-squared values, suggesting a strong influence upon life satisfaction, job satisfaction, and job performance. Others skills had R-squared values close to zero, meaning that particular skill had essentially no influence upon job and life satisfaction and job performance outcomes. By comparing the R-squared values yielded by each of the twenty-six soft-skill competencies in the study, we were able to discover the unique variance explained by these skills, and determine which skill was the most important to success. Standardized beta coefficients were used to assess the significance of the relationship between each soft skill and job performance, job satisfaction, and life satisfaction. The relative predictive power of the twenty-six soft skills was assessed by converting standardized beta coefficients to Z scores. This enabled a ranking system that considered the relative influence of all twenty-six skills on job performance, job satisfaction, and life satisfaction collectively. Some of the twenty-six skills had little connection to these outcomes—that is, they had little influence on them—while others had a modest to strong influence. Self-awareness had a strong influence on these outcomes and ranked first among the twenty-six—it was the most critical skill. This finding is important, given that discovering your personality profile is the most direct path to increasing your self-awareness. A complete ranking of the twenty-six soft-skill competencies based on their relative influence on these outcomes follows. Those soft-skill competencies that had no significant influence on these outcomes are listed at the bottom of the table, in the shaded area.

Soft Skill	Rank
Self-Awareness	1
Relationship Management	2
Courage	3
Self-Management	4
Communication	5
Planning	6
Acumen	7
Vision	8
Risk-Taking	9
Rehearsal	10
Flexibility	11
Values Differences	12
Research	13
Decision-Making	14
Teamwork	15
Results-Focus	16
Mobilizing Others	17
Lifelong Learning	18
Social Awareness	19
Integrity	20
Rules	21
Credibility	22
Information-Sharing	23
Outcome Concern	24
Building Commitment	25
Empowerment	26

Acknowledgments

The body of research behind this book is the result of a tremendous effort by the bright and dedicated team of behavioral scientists at TalentSmart®. I'm extremely grateful for the opportunity to write about these findings, and it would not be possible without their time, energy, and tireless dedication. They make it all worthwhile. Specifically, I'd like to acknowledge the leadership and dedication of Lac Su, Jean Riley, Tanya Goodwin-Maslach, Alexandria Herrera, and Nick Tasler. On behalf of everyone at TalentSmart, I offer special thanks to Yufan Chen, programmer extraordinaire, and his talented team of coders, network engineers, and thinkers. We couldn't move an inch without their all-nighters. I also thank Jean Greaves for being a wonderful business partner, mentor, and friend. We are deeply indebted to the people who participated in our research and let us look into their lives during the last decade, and we admire their willingness to share themselves in the name of learning and scientific discovery.

To Michele Tarlo and the entire team at CruxCreative.com, what can I say but *"Wow!"* I couldn't be happier with the book's illustrations and website. Once again, you've far exceeded my wildest expectations with your proficiency in creating a fabulous, synergized look for every aspect of the concept—from start to finish—and for *never* missing a deadline.

A heartfelt thank-you to John Duff at Putnam for supporting this project and providing thorough, insightful editorial direction. Our work together on this book is living proof that an Entrepreneur and a Diplomat can align their efforts with synergy and harmony. Thanks also to assistant editor Jeanette Shaw, Summer Smith and the publicity team, Amy C. King for the jacket design, Nicole LaRoche for the interior design, Leda Scheintaub for the copy editing, and the entire team at Putnam who brought this book to life.

I'm grateful to have received invaluable feedback that improved earlier versions of this manuscript, the IDISC Personality Profiler, and the factual content explored within each, from the following: Paul Brooks, Matt and Kelly Baier, Josh Feder, Kirsti and Mel Senac, Sommer Kerhli, Michael Schmidt, Michele Tarlo, Bruce Evans, Jeff Cohen, Tracey Gunner, Elise Freemont, Stacy Ramirez, Lac Su, Tanya Goodwin-Maslach, Nick and Alison Tasler, Jean Riley, Alexandria Herrera, Jean Greaves, Cathy Hemming, Julia Serebrinsky, George Grant, Monica Saare, Leslie Wilson, Shira Oretzky, Jenny Tsoulos, Scott Harris, Isabel Peraza, Humberto Peraza, Jr., Les Brown, Bob Maslach, and Angelica Barragan. As a writer, you're only as good as what you put on paper, and improving your words requires people who take the time to read and consider your work. In my young writing career, I've had the opportunity to receive this support from the following individuals, whom I thank for their time and their support of my work: H. H. the Dalai Lama, Ken Blanchard,

Stephen Covey, Patrick Lencioni, Lois Frankel, Matt Olmstead, Captain Michael D. Abrashoff, Joseph Grenny, Jim Loehr, Brian Tracy, Dr. Beverly Kaye, and Marshall Goldsmith.

A very big thank-you to my agent, Steve Hanselman, and the team at LevelFiveMedia for supporting this book from the very beginning and working so hard to refine the idea and find the right publisher. I sincerely appreciate Steve's willingness to work so closely with me and share his wealth of experience turning good ideas into great books. The agency is a joy to work with, and a real rarity in publishing today.

A final note of appreciation to my wonderful wife for supporting my insatiable pursuit of this writing thing. Irregular hours, caffeine, and harebrained ideas are the tools of a trade that requires a great deal of genuine empathy to tolerate, let alone care for the person engaged in it. Somehow you do it, and I'm deeply grateful for that. I love you.

Notes

Introduction: Separated at Birth

The story of Thomas Patterson and Steven Tazumi was covered by the media in various places shortly after they were reunited in July 1999. See Associated Press, "Twins Being Reunited After Separation as Babies," *Chanute Tribune* (Kansas), July 13, 1999; and Debra and Lisa Ganz, "Twins Separated at Birth in Japan Reunited 40 Years Later," available at www.twinsworld.com/news_archive. A transcript of an interview with Thomas Patterson and Steve Tazumi on Fred Goodwin's radio show *The Infinite Mind* of February 9, 2000, is available at http://lcmedia.com/mindprgm.htm.

Though the situation has improved to some degree since the 1950s, single mothers are subject to considerable discrimination in Japanese culture. For more on the subject, see Megan McKinlay, "Unstable Mothers: Redefining Motherhood in Contemporary Japan," *Intersections* 7 (March 2002). The article is available online at wwwsshe.murdoch.edu.au/intersections/issue7/mckinlay.html.

For a discussion of physical anomalies between genetically identical twins, see Nancy Segal's *Entwined Lives* (New York: Dutton, 1999).

The incredible similarities between identical twins Steve Tazumi and Tom Patterson are bound to lead to thoughts of the age-old nature versus nurture debate. That is, because they are so incredibly similar, does that mean our behavior and our appearance are solely dictated by our genetics? While this was a concern to psychological science in decades past, the research published in the last fifteen to twenty years is conclusive: Who we are behaviorally is controlled 50% by our genes and 50% by our environment. While genetically identical twins usually look incredibly similar, their behavior often varies. In the case of Tom and Steve, their environments lined up in such a way during their development that their personalities and, by definition, much of their behavior were uncannily similar. For a complete explanation of the differential impact of our genes and our environment on our behavior, see Nancy Segal's second book on twins, *Indivisible by Two* (Cambridge, MA: Harvard University Press, 2005).

For other findings from the TalentSmart study, see Travis Bradberry and Jean Greaves, *The Emotional Intelligence Quick Book: Everything You Need to Know to Put Your EQ to Work* (New York: Simon & Schuster, 2005).

For a look at some of the other skills measured by the TalentSmart study, of which emotional intelligence has garnered the most media attention, see Travis Bradberry and Jean Greaves, "Heartless Bosses," *Harvard Business Review,* December 2005, and Martha Brant, "Why Emotional Intelligence Matters," *Newsweek.com,* June 14, 2005, msnbc.msn.com/id/8214937/site/newsweek/.

A detailed discourse on how the pathways for thinking (neural pathways) in the brain are formed is found in Joseph LeDoux, *Synaptic Self: How Our Brains Become Who We Are* (New York: Penguin, 2002).

An interesting window to the permanence of the hardwired pathways for thinking in the brain is seen in physiological studies of trauma. During these intensely traumatic experiences, neural pathways are damaged. See the work of Harvard psychologist B. A. van der Kolk, "The Body Keeps the Score: Memory and the Emerging Psychobiology of Post Traumatic Stress," *Harvard Review of Psychiatry,* 1 (1994):

253–265. B. A. van der Kolk et al., "Dissociation, Somatization, and Affect Dysregulation: The Complexity of Adaptation of Trauma," *American Journal of Psychiatry, 153* (1996): 83–93.

The permanence of personality is revealed by longitudinal studies, which track the same individuals over the course of years and measure the change, or, as the case is, a lack thereof. For longitudinal studies conducted by unique sets of researchers who've reached similar conclusions as to the stability of personality, see P. T. Costa, Jr., E. J. Metter, and R. R. McCrae, "Personality Stability and Its Contribution to Successful Aging," *Journal of Geriatric Psychiatry*, 27 (1994): 40–59. J. Block and J. H. Block, "Venturing a 30-Year Longitudinal Study," *American Psychologist*, 61, 4 (2006): 315–327. J. J. Conley, "A Personality Theory of Adulthood and Aging, in R. Hogan and W. Jones, eds., *Perspectives in Personality,* vol. 1 (Greenwich, CT: JAI Press, 1985). S. Soldz and G. E. Vaillant, "The Big Five Personality Traits and the Life Course: A 45-Year Longitudinal Study," *Journal of Research in Personality, 33* (1999): 208–232.

The fourteen personality types, including how they were derived, are discussed at length in this book. However, there is more information on the subject, in the form of a pair of free, downloadable white papers titled "IDISC: Therefore I Am" and "The Business Case for Personality," at www.talentsmart.com/learn.

The number of possible personality configurations is based on a series of calculations that considers the quantity of personality characteristics measured and the degrees of variability available within each personality characteristic. See T. Pappas, "Pascal's Triangle, the Fibonacci Sequence and Binomial Formula" and "Probability and Pascal's Triangle," in *The Joy of Mathematics* (San Carlos, CA: Wide World, 1989).

1: The Anatomy of Personality

More information on the design of the Baltimore Longitudinal Study of Aging, and its founders, can be found online at www.grc.nia.nih.gov/branches/blsa/blsanew.htm.

The increase in vocabulary that occurs for people well into their eighties, as discovered by the Baltimore Study of Aging, is documented by L. M. Giambra et al., "Adult Life Span Changes in Immediate Visual Memory and Verbal Intelligence," *Psychology of Aging*, 10 (1995): 123–139.

For more on the impact of aging on metabolism, as discovered by the Baltimore Longitudinal Study of Aging, see the transcript of Australian Broadcasting Corporation's *The Health Report* of July 14, 1997; available at www.abc.net.au/rn/talks/8.30/helthrpt/stories/s179.htm. Also see R. E. Vestal et al., "Aging and Ethanol Metabolism," *Clinical Pharmacology and Therapeutics*, 21 (1977): 343–354.

Quotations from Fred Litwin on his experience in the Baltimore Longitudinal Study of Aging appear in Janet Silver, "Baltimore Longitudinal Study on Ageing," ABC (Australia) *The Health Report*, July 14, 1997; found online at www. abc. net .aa/rn/talks/ 8.30/helthrpt/stories/s179.htm.

The story of Fred Litwin's elevator—which uses man-powered pulleys as opposed to an engine, and was the first model with a safety device to prevent riders from plummeting to the basement upon equipment failure—is found in Marjorie Hunter, "Case Study for Elevator Antiquarians," *New York Times*, May 6, 1985.

At the time of publication, the state of Fred Litwin's elevator—the oldest known original in the United States—is uncertain at best. His furniture shop, formerly located at the intersection of Indiana Avenue, Pennsylvania, 7th Street, and C Alley in downtown Washington, D.C., across from the Temperance Fountain, is now closed. See John Kelly, "John Kelly's Washington Live," *Washington Post Online*, May 20, 2005, http://www.washingtonpost.com/wp-dyn/content/discussion/2005/05/13/DI200505130116.

Gail Sheehy's immensely popular self-help book *Passages: Predictable Crises of Adult Life* (New York: Dutton, 1976) proposed the influence of life stages on personality development, which dominated the public's perception of personality during this time. It went on to sell more than six million copies, influenced the media's adoption of the term "midlife crisis," and continued the mistaken belief that personality fluctuates throughout our lifetimes. Other publications of note that influenced the public's perception that personality changes through life stages include George E. Vaillant, *Adaptation to Life* (Boston: Little, Brown, 1977); Roger L. Gould, *Transformations* (New York: Simon & Schuster, 1978); and Daniel J. Levinson, *The Seasons of a Woman's Life* (New York: Knopf, 1996).

Dr. Paul T. Costa is quoted in the interview with Fred Litwin from ABC's *The Health Report* (see earlier notes), and from his book with Robert R. McCrae, *Personality in Adulthood: A Five-Factor Theory Perspective* (New York: Guilford, 2003).

Accounts of Terry Wallis's accident and recovery are seen in Benedict Cary, "Mute 19 Years, He Helps Reveal Brain's Mysteries," *New York Times,* July 4, 2006; and "Arkansan's Brain Grew New Nerves," *Arkansas Democrat Gazette,* July 4, 2006.

Individuals who had difficult recoveries from a position similar to Terry's are described by Sam Lister in "Miracle of Crash Victim Who Awoke After 19 Years in a Coma," *The Times* (London), July 4, 2006.

Those interested in helping the family of Terry Wallis to help fund his extensive care should contact: Terry Wallis Special Needs Trust, Bank of Izard County, P.O. Box 1999, Mountain View, AR 72560.

Detailed findings of the team from Cornell who've observed Terry Wallis appear in Henning U. Voss et al., "Possible Axonal Regrowth in Late Recovery from the Minimally Conscious State," *The Journal of Clinical Investigation,* 116, 7 (July 2006): 2005–2111.

A stellar summary of the cerebellum's role as a processing center coordinating various regions of the brain is Henrietta C. Leiner and Alan Leiner, "The Treasure at the

Bottom of the Brain," which can be found at www.newhorizons.org/neuro/
leiner.htm. Also see Eric Courchesne and Greg Allen, "Prediction and Preparation,
Fundamental Functions of the Cerebellum," *Learning and Memory,* 4: 1 (May/June
1997): 1–35.

For more information on brain plasticity, see the landmark article that introduced
the term, by T. P. Pons et al., "Massive Cortical Reorganization After Sensory De-
afferentation in Adult Macaques, *Science,* 252 (November 13, 1992): 1159–1160;
N. Jain, "Deactivation and Reactivation of Somatosensory Cortex Is Accompanied
by Reductions in GABA Straining," *Somatosensory and Motor Research,* 8 (1997):
347–354. D. Borsook et al., "Acute Plasticity in the Human Somatosensory Cortex
Following Amputation," *NeuroReport,* 9 (1998): 1013–1017.

For more on the neuroplasticity of personality early in life, see E. R. Kandel, J. H.
Schwartz, and T. M. Jessell, *Essentials of Neural Sciences and Behavior* (Stamford,
CT: Appleton and Lange, 1995); and C. J. Shatz, "The Developing Brain," in Read-
ings from Scientific American: *Mind and Brain* (New York: Freeman, 1993), 15–26.

For more on the number and structure of neurons in the brain, see *The Scientific
American Book of the Brain,* 3rd ed. (New York: Scientific American, 1999); E. R.
Kandel, J. H. Schwartz, and T. M. Jessell, *Principles of Neural Science,* 4th ed.
(New York: McGraw-Hill, 2000).

For further exploration of the physical changes to the central nervous system that
are initiated by environmental influences, see C. H. Bailey and E. R. Kandel,
"Structural Changes Accompanying Memory Storage," *Annual Review of Physiology,* 55 (1993): 397–426.

Regarding the discovery of the location of personality in the right orbitalfrontal
cortex of the brain, see interviews with Robert T. Knight, of the University of California at Berkeley, and Michael Gazzaniga, of Dartmouth College, in the video *Studying the Mind* (New York: Norton, 2003; www.wwnorten.com/psychsci/content/
video_exercises/ch08.asp).

The research studying the frontal lobe brain development in children at the Shriver Center in Massachusetts sets a high standard for the matching of behavioral phenomena against simultaneous scanning of the brain. The research discussed here was seen in the Frontiers television program 1302, *Make Up Your Mind,* produced by *Scientific American* magazine, which premiered on October 15, 2002.

The medical theories of Hippocrates historically are represented in the *Hippocratic Corpus,* a collection of ancient Greek medical works. Hippocrates is considered the author of some, but not all, of the texts in this work. Though it cannot be determined with certainty which works were penned by Hippocrates himself, the thinking cited in this chapter comes from works that are attributed by most scholars to Hippocrates. A direct translation of the entire *Hippocratic Corpus* is available online at http://classics.mit.edu/Browse/browse-Hippocrates.html. An excellent book that contains writings attributed to Hippocrates, as well as a fuller picture of ancient Greek medicine that spans centuries and represents broader works generally attributed to other Greek thinkers, is *Hippocratic Writings* (New York: Penguin, 1984).

The Hippocratic Corpus quite literally predominated thinking in medicine through the Middle Ages. Certain practices produced by this theory, such as bloodletting, continued to be practiced through the American Civil War in the 1860s. On this historical influence of Hippocrates on the practice of medicine, see Vivian Nutton, *Ancient Medicine* (New York: Routledge, 2004), and Lawrence Conrad, Michael Neve, Vivian Nutton, Roy Porter, and Andrew Wear, *The Western Medical Tradition: 800 B.C. to A.D. 1800* (New York: Cambridge University Press, 1995).

The oath taken by physicians is a sign of the place of Hippocratic theory in medicine, and the progression of this oath can be seen in M. B. Etziony's *The Physician's Creed: An Anthology of Medical Prayers, Oaths, and Codes of Ethics Written and Recited by Medical Practitioners Through the Ages* (Springfield, MA: Charles C. Thomas, 1973).

William James was the Harvard professor who influenced William Marston, and is considered the first American psychologist. James taught medicine, physiology, and biology at Harvard at a time when the study of the human mind was yet to be identified as a science. He pioneered the field of psychology by integrating his knowledge of these subjects into the study of the mind. His influential books include *The Principles of Psychology* (Mineola, NY: Dover, 1950), *The Will to Believe* (Mineola, NY: Dover, 1956), *Human Immortality* (Mineola, NY: Dover, 1956), and *The Meaning of Truth* (Kila, MT: Kessinger, 2004). A comprehensive look at his early works is found in *William James: Writings 1878–1889: Psychology, Briefer Course, The Will to Believe, Talks to Teachers and Students,* and *Essays* (New York: Library of America, 1992).

Skin conductivity is measured through the galvanic skin response—a measure of electrical resistance produced by emotional arousal that is taken by attaching electrodes to any part of the skin and recording changes in moment-to-moment activity related to the autonomic nervous system—an addition to the polygraph post-Marston that has continued as a benchmark of the body's physiological response to emotion. For more, see Yashura Kimoshi, Aihide Yoshino, Yoshimoto Takahashi, and Sichiro Nomura, "Interhemispheric Difference in Emotional Response Without Awareness," *Physiology and Behavior,* 82, 4 (September 30, 2004): 727–731: K. H. Kim, S. W. Bang, and S. R. Kim, "Emotion Recognition System Using Short-Term Monitoring of Physiological Signals," *Medical & Biological Engineering & Computing,* 42, 3 (2004): 419–427. Witvliet VanOyen, Charlotte Vrana, and R. Scott, "Psychophysiological Responses as Indices of Affective Dimensions," *Psychophysiology,* 32, 5 (1995): 436–443.

Other physiological measures have added to the sophistication of the polygraph. For more on this, see Richard I. Thackray and Martin T. Orne, "A Comparison of Physiological Indices in Detection of Deception," *Psychophysiology,* 4, 3 (1968): 329–339; and John A. Podlesny and David C. Raskin, "Effectiveness of Techniques and Physiological Measures in the Detection of Deception," *Psychophysiology,* 15, 4 (1978): 344–359.

More information on Marston's development of the technique behind the polygraph is found in the following works that highlight the physiological responses of the body when a person lies: William Moulton Marston, "Reaction Time Symptoms of Deception," *Journal of Experimental Psychology,* 3 (1926): 72–87; William Moulton Marston, "Systolic Blood Pressure Symptoms of Deception and Constituent Mental States" (Ph.D. thesis, Harvard University, 1921); William Moulton Marston, "Psychological Possibilities in the Deception Tests," *Journal of Criminal Law and Criminology,* 11, 4 (February 1921): 112–131; William Marston, *The Lie Detector Test* (New York: Smith, 1938); and P. L. Harriman, ed., "Lie Detection's Bodily Basis and Test Procedures," in *Encyclopedia of Psychology* (New York: Oxford University Press, 1947).

People lie far more frequently than they realize. The study that shows that a little over half of us admit to lying yet 97% lie when tracked comes from the Associated Press, July 11, 2006. Other studies show that the average person tells a lie at least once a day. For more on the topic, see Peter Doskotch, "The Real Truth About Lying," *Psychology Today,* 29, 5 (September/October 1996): 16; and Elizabeth B. Ford, "Lie Detection: Historical, Neuropsychiatric and Legal Dimensions," *International Journal of Law and Psychiatry,* 29, 3 (May/June 2006): 159–177.

For more on Marston's connection between the body's physiological responses to emotion and personality, see William Moulton Marston, "Primary Emotions," *Psychological Review,* 34 (1927): 336–363; William Moulton Marston, "Motor Consciousness as a Basis for Emotion," *Journal of Abnormal and Social Psychology,* 22 (1927): 140–150; and William Moulton Marston, "Bodily Symptoms of Elementary Emotions," *Psyche,* 10 (1929): 70–86.

When Marston unveiled his model of personality, the work of Sigmund Freud and Carl Jung dominated the world's conception of the human psyche. Both Freud and Jung postulated that human behavior was the result of unconscious conflicts, and Marston saw two major flaws in this thinking. First, he found the dynamics of unconscious conflicts unwieldy—it was impractical for the average person to understand and reap any benefit from them. Second, they weren't based on any research. To learn more about his original DISC model of personality, see his book *The Emotions of Normal People* (New York: Taylor & Francis, 1928).

Marston's DISC model was first developed into an assessment in 1977 at the University of Minnesota, in a project led by John G. Geier. For more on this, see William Moulton Marston, *The Emotions of Normal People: Introduced with an Interpretation, References, and a Presentation of a New Construct—Situation Perception Analysis—by John G. Geier, Ph.D.* (Minneapolis: Persona Press, 1979). This test is often referred to as the Personal Profile System, or Disc Classic, which is published by Inscape Publishing. The Inscape Disc test is responsible for introducing more than forty million people to Marston's DISC personality model. For more on this, see Julie Straw, *The 4-Dimensional Manager: Disc® Strategies for Managing Different People in the Best Ways* (San Francisco: Berrett-Koehler, 2002).

Later in his career, Dr. William Marston's work moved away from psychological research and more into vehicles that had the public's attention. His development of the Wonder Woman comic book character was a product of his speculation that women would achieve greater autonomy in the coming decades, and children needed an assertive, self-directed female role model. For more on this, see William Moulton Marston, "Why 100,000,000 Americans Read Comics," *The American Scholar,* 13, 1 (1944): 35–44; Geoffrey C. Bunn, "The Lie Detector, *Wonder Woman,* and Liberty: The Life and Works of William Moulton Marston," *The History of the Human Sciences,* 10 (1997): 91–119; and Les Daniels and Chip Kidd, *Wonder Woman: A Complete History* (San Francisco: Chronicle, 2000).

2: Self-Awareness Breeds Success

The secret to Michael Larson's success on *Press Your Luck* was first revealed in an interview with *TV Guide* in November 1994, "The Day the Game Show Got Whammied." Subsequent coverage included Associated Press, "Metro Ohioan Pulled 'Whammy' to Win on Game Show," November 28, 1994. The most thorough coverage of his life after the show—including the first airing on television in more than a decade of the *Press Your Luck* episodes in which he appeared—comes from a 2003 documentary on the Game Show Network, "Big Bucks: The Press Your Luck Scandal." Finally, a website dedicated to the show will answer most any question you could have about Michael Larson and *Press Your Luck*: http://gscentral.net/pyl.htm.

The understanding of self-awareness as a critical component of emotional intelligence comes from the first significant studies in the field at Yale University. These include Jack Mayer et al., "Perceiving Affective Content in Ambiguous Visual Stimuli: A Component of Emotional Intelligence," *Journal of Personality Assessment,* 54 (1990); Jack Mayer and Peter Salovey, "The Intelligence of Emotional Intelligence." *Intelligence,* 17 (1993); and Jack Mayer and A. Stevens, "An Emerging Understanding of the Reflective (Meta) Experience of Mood," *Journal of Research in Personality,* 28 (1994).

For further discussion of the location of personality in a separate region of the brain, see Donald T. Stuss and Robert T. Knight, *Principles of Frontal Lobe Function* (New York: Oxford University Press, 2002). Summaries of Knight's latest research and new and forthcoming articles are found at http://psychology.berkeley.edu/faculty/ profiles/rknight.html. Dr. Michael Gazzaniga is the director of Cognitive Neuroscience at Dartmouth, whose research is mentioned regarding the separation of emotional and personality functions in the brain's prefrontal cortex. His studies exploring how the brain enables the mind can be found at www.dartmouth.edu/~cogneuro/ Gazzaniga.html.

For details on the history and use of psychological testing, see Robert J. Gregory, *Psychological Testing: History, Principles, and Applications,* 4th ed. (New York: Allyn & Bacon, 2003).

The accuracy of personality assessment via self-report is a phenomena based on the finding that self-reports increase in accuracy with the width of the behavior set that is being measured. See S. Epstein, "Traits Are Alive and Well," in David Magnusson and Norman S. Endler, eds., *Personality at the Crossroads: Current Issues in Interactional Psychology* (Hillsdale, NJ: Erlbaum, 1987) 83–98. Similar findings were subsequently reported by D. S. Moskowitz, "Cross-Situational Generality in the Laboratory: Dominance and Friendliness," *The Journal of Personality and Social Psychology,* 54 (1988): 829–839; and D. C. Funder and C. D. Sneed, "Behavioral Manifestations of Personality: An Ecological Approach to Judgmental Accuracy," *The Journal of Personality and Social Psychology,* 64 (1993): 479–490.

Though this book is the first to publish the full scope and implications of the TalentSmart study, the magnitude of its accumulated findings have lent themselves to a variety of publications since the findings were first revealed a few years ago. For the most detailed description of the findings early in the study, see Travis Bradberry and Jean Greaves, *The Emotional Intelligence Quick Book: Everything You Need to Know to Put Your EQ to Work* (New York: Simon & Schuster, 2005).

Data on the link between self-awareness, as a component of emotional intelligence, and job performance is seen in Travis Bradberry, *The Business Case for Emotional Intelligence,* which is available for download at www.talentsmart.com/media/uploads/pdfs/The_Business_Case_For_EQ.pdf.

For the negative impact of a lack of self-awareness beyond the TalentSmart study, see O. Ayduk and W. Mischel, "When Smart People Behave Stupidly: Reconciling Inconsistencies in Social-Emotional Intelligence," in Robert J. Sternberg, ed., *Why Smart People Can Be So Stupid* (New Haven, CT: Yale University Press, 2002).

For the impact of self-awareness on fundamental concerns like happiness and life satisfaction beyond the findings of the TalentSmart study, see Marc A. Brackett et al., "Emotional Intelligence and Its Relation to Everyday Behavior," *Personality and Individual Differences,* 36 (2004): 1387–1402. Benjamin Palmer et al., "Emotional Intelligence and Life Satisfaction," *Personality and Individual Differences,* 33 (2002): 1091–1100; and Adrian Furnham, "Trait Emotional Intelligence and Happiness," *Social Behavior & Personality* 31 (2003): 815–824.

The vast majority of the validity data on the IDISC assessment is published in Appendix A of this book; additional information be found in a "Fact Sheet" for the test at www.talentsmart.com/media/uploads/pdfs/iDISC_Fact_Sheet.pdf.

3: The IDISC Personality Profiler

For more on the complexity of functions controlled by the brain, see Shannon Moffett, *The Three-Pound Enigma* (New York: Workman, 2006), Joseph LeDoux, *The Emotional Brain: The Mysterious Underpinnings of Emotional Life* (New York: Simon & Schuster, 2006).

For more on measuring the function of the heart, see Ricardo Oliveira et al., "Influence of Different Respiratory Maneuvers on Exercise-Induced Cardiac Vagal Inhibition," *European Journal of Applied Physiology*, 97, 5 (June 10, 2006): 607–612.

On the act of solidifying behavior change through active and objective guidance, see Thomas L. Webb and Paschal Sheeran, "Does Changing Behavioral Intentions Engender Behavior Change? A Meta-Analysis of the Experimental Evidence," *Psychological Bulletin*, 132, 2 (2006): 249–268.

For the article on the perils of personality testing, see Barbara Ehrenreich, "Boys Just Want to Have Fun," *Time*, July 23, 2006.

For the *New York Times* article on the public's misattribution of personality to genetic factors of behavior, see Amy Harmon, "That Wild Streak? Maybe It Runs in the Family," *New York Times*, June 15, 2006.

Broad concerns as to the psychometric validity of instruments that are commonly considered to be measures of personality are seen in Annie M. Paul, *The Cult of Personality: How Personality Tests Are Leading Us to Miseducate Our Children, Mismanage Our Companies, and Misunderstand Ourselves* (New York: Free Press, 2004).

A targeted discussion of the psychometric concerns of assessments commonly used to measure personality include David J. Pittenger, "Measuring the MBTI and Coming Up Short," *Journal of Career Planning & Placement*, Fall 1993: 48–53.

For more on the tracking functions of the goal-tracking system, see Travis Bradberry and Jean Greaves, "Can You Develop Emotional Intelligence Online?" *Learning and Training Innovations* (December 2003). The importance of setting goals and the power of making goals public are discussed in Francis Hesselbein et al., *The Leader of the Future* (San Francisco: Jossey-Bass, 1997).

On the superiority of the objectivity provided by assessments, see L. E. Atwater, C. Ostroff, F. J. Yammarino, and J. W. Fleenor, "Self–Other Agreement: Does It Really Matter?" *Personnel Psychology,* 51 (1998): 577–598; and L. E. Atwater and F. J. Yammarino, "Does Self–Other Agreement on Leadership Perceptions Moderate the Validity of Leadership and Performance Predictors?" *Personnel Psychology,* 45 (1992): 141–155.

4: The Fourteen Types of People

For more on Shaquille O'Neal, see Shaquille O'Neal, *Shaq Talks Back* (New York: St. Martin's, 2002), and Phil Jackson, *The Last Season: A Team in Search of Its Soul* (New York: Penguin, 2004).

Though most NBA games are held in arenas that hold 20,000 to 30,000 people, several games have been held in venues drawing more than 30,000 people. See Associated Press, "35,184 See Pistons Top Bucks," *New York Times,* April 1, 1984; and "April 13, 1990 in History," *Brainy History,* www.brainyhistory.com/events/1990/april_13_1990_163460.html.

The account of NBA referee Bob Delaney's work infiltrating the mob comes from "The NBA Half Time Report" on ABC during game two of the 2006 NBA finals between the Dallas Mavericks and the Miami Heat. For more on his story, see Chris Anderson, "Whistle-blower: Bob Delaney Goes from Undercover Cop to NBA Referee," *Sarasota Herald-Tribune,* March 8, 2006.

The representation of Lucille Ball as an Ally is based on my compilation of her personality as derived from the mountains of information on her life. For more on her, see Lucille Ball, *Love, Lucy* (New York: Berkley, 1997); Kathleen Brady, *Lucille: The Life of Lucille Ball* (New York: Watson-Guptill Publications, 2000); and Coyne S. Sanders and Tom Gilbert, *Desilu: The Story of Lucille Ball and Desi Arnaz* (New York: Harper, 1994).

Johnny Carson is represented as an Ally on the basis of details of his life provided in Ed McMahon, *Here's Johnny! My Memories of Johnny Carson, The Tonight Show, and 46 Years of Friendship* (Nashville: Rutledge, 2005), and Laurence Leamer, *King of the Night: The Life of Johnny Carson* (New York: Avon, 2005).

George Lucas is represented as an Architect on the basis of discussions with members of the George Lucas Educational Foundation and information in Dale Pollock, *Skywalking: The Life and Films of George Lucas* (New York, Da Capo, 1999), George Lucas and Sally Kline, *George Lucas: Interviews* (Jackson: University Press of Mississippi, 1999).

My description of Charles Schulz as an Architect is based on Rheta Grimsley Johnson, *Good Grief: The Story of Charles M. Schulz* (Kansas City: Andrews McMeel, 1995); Jim Whiting, *Charles Schulz* (Hockessin, DE: Mitchell Lane, 2002); and "Peanuts Fans Mourn Death of Creator, Charles Schulz," CNN.com, February 13, 2000, http://archives.cnn.com/2000/US/02/13/schulz.obit.02/index.html.

My description of Phil Jackson as a Coach is based on Phil Jackson, *Sacred Hoops: Spiritual Lessons of a Hardwood Warrior* (New York: Hyperion, 1996), and Phil Jackson and Michael Arkush, *The Last Season: A Team in Search of Its Soul* (New York: Penguin, 2004).

My description of Peter Drucker as a Coach is based on *The Essential Drucker: The Best of Sixty Years of Peter Drucker's Essential Writings on Management* (New York: Collins, 2003), and on Drucker's *The Practice of Management* (New York: Collins, 1993).

My description of Thomas Edison as a Detective is based on Matthew Josephson, *Edison: A Biography* (New York: Wiley, 1992), and Paul Israel, *Edison: A Life of Invention* (New York: Wiley, 2000).

My description of Albert Einstein as a Detective is based on the definitive biography of his life and work by Abraham Pais, *Subtle Is the Lord: The Science and the Life of Albert Einstein* (Oxford: Oxford University Press, 2002), and Roger Highfield and Paul Carter, *The Private Lives of Albert Einstein* (Boston: Faber & Faber, 1994).

My description of Desmond Tutu as a Diplomat is based on his book *God Has a Dream: A Vision of Hope for Our Time* (New York: Doubleday, 2004), and Steven D. Gish, *Desmond Tutu: A Biography* (Westport, CT: Greenwood, 2004).

My description of His Holiness the Dalai Lama as a Diplomat is based on his books *The Universe in a Single Atom: The Convergence of Science and Spirituality* (New York: Morgan Road, 2005), and *The Art of Happiness: A Handbook for Living,* written with Howard C. Cutler (New York: Riverhead, 1998).

My description of Bill Gates as an Entrepreneur is based on Stephen Manes and Paul Andrews, *Gates: How Microsoft's Mogul Reinvented an Industry—and Made Himself the Richest Man in America* (New York: Touchstone, 1994), and Janet Lowe, *Bill Gates Speaks: Insights from the World's Greatest Entrepreneur* (New York: Wiley, 2001).

My description of César Chávez, an Entrepreneur, is based on Susan Ferriss and Ricardo Sandoval, *The Fight in the Fields: Cesar Chavez and the Farmworkers Movement,* ed. Diana Hembree (New York: Harvest, 1998), and Frederick John Dalton, *The Moral Vision of César Chávez* (Maryknoll: Orbis, 2003).

My description of Jane Goodall as an Expert is based on her books *Through a Window: My Thirty Years Observing the Gombe Chimpanzees* (Boston: Houghton Mifflin, 1990), and *Reason for Hope: A Spiritual Journey,* written with Phillip Berman (New York: Warner, 1999).

My description of George Washington Carver as an Expert is based on Gary R. Kremer, ed., *George Washington Carver in His Own Words* (Columbia: University of Missouri Press, 1987).

My description of Elvis Presley as an Innovator is based on Elaine Dundy, *Elvis and Gladys* (New York: St. Martin's, 2001), and Peter Guralnick, *Lost Train to Memphis: The Rise of Elvis Presley* (New York: Back Bay, 1995).

My description of Pablo Picasso as an Innovator is based on Patrick O'Brian, *Picasso: A Biography* (New York: Norton, 1994).

My description of Oprah Winfrey as a Mobilizer is based on Janet Lowe, *Oprah Winfrey Speaks* (New York: Wiley, 2001), and Bill Adler, ed., *The Uncommon Wisdom of Oprah Winfrey: A Portrait in Her Own Words* (New York: Carol, 1997).

My description of John F. Kennedy as a Mobilizer is based on Michael O' Brien, *John F. Kennedy: A Biography* (New York: St. Martin's, 2005), and the Pulitzer Prize–winning book by Kennedy's close advisor Arthur Schlesinger, Jr., and David Sobel, *A Thousand Days: John F. Kennedy in the White House* (New York: Black Dog & Leventhal, 2005).

My description of Ronald Reagan as a Motivator is based on Reagan's *An American Life: Ronald Reagan* (New York: Simon & Schuster, 1990), and Dinesh D'Souza, *Ronald Reagan: How an Ordinary Man Became an Extraordinary Leader* (New York: Fireside, 1999).

My description of Jesse Jackson as a Motivator is based on Marshall Frady, *Jesse Jackson: A Biography* (New York: Random House, 1996).

My description of Teddy Roosevelt as an Opportunist is based on Kathleen Dalton, *Theodore Roosevelt: A Strenuous Life* (New York: Knopf, 2002), and H. W. Brands, *The Selected Letters of Theodore Roosevelt* (Whitestone, NY: Cooper Square, 2001).

My description of Henry Ford as an Opportunist is based on Anne Jardim, *The First Henry Ford: A Study in Personality and Business Leadership* (Cambridge, MA: Massachusetts Institute of Technology Press, 1970), and Richard Bak, *Henry and Edsel: The Creation of the Ford Empire* (New York: Wiley, 2003).

My description of Warren Buffett as a Researcher is based on Amanda Cantrell, "Buffett Calls Wealth Giveaway 'Logical,'" CNN.com, June 26, 2006, and Bernard Ryan, Jr., *Warren Buffett: Financier* (New York: Ferguson, 2005).

My description of Jonas Salk as a Researcher is based on Jeffrey Kluger, *Splendid Solution: Jonas Salk and the Conquest of Polio* (New York: Putnam, 2005).

My description of George Burns as a Sponsor is based on Herb Fagen and George Burns, *George Burns: In His Own Words* (New York: Carroll & Graf, 1996), and Martin Gottfried, *George Burns* (New York: Simon & Schuster, 1996).

My description of Shaquille O'Neal as a Sponsor is based on his book *Shaq Talks Back: The Uncensored Word on My Life and Winning in the NBA* (New York: St. Martin's, 2001), and Matt Christopher and Glenn Stout, *On the Court with . . . Shaquille O'Neal* (New York: Little, Brown, 2003).

My description of George S. Patton as a Strategist is based on David Andrew Smith, *George S. Patton: A Biography* (Westport, CT: Greenwood, 2003), and George S. Patton and Rick Atkinson, *War As I Knew It* (New York: Mariner, 1995).

My description of Vince Lombardi as a Strategist is based on David Maraniss, *When Pride Still Mattered: A Life of Vince Lombardi* (New York: Simon & Schuster, 2000), and Don Phillips, *Run to Win: Vince Lombardi on Coaching and Leadership* (New York: St. Martin's, 2002).

Epilogue: Moving Forward

For more on Marston's development of the Wonder Woman comic book character, see his article "Why 100,000,000 Americans Read Comics," *The American Scholar,* 13 (1944): 35–44.

Appendix A: Inside the IDISC

The standards for assessment development and validation as set forth by the American Psychological Association can be found in its *Standards for Educational and Psychological Testing* (Washington, DC: American Psychological Association, 1999).

To learn more about his original DISC model of personality, see William Marston's *The Emotions of Normal People* (New York: Taylor & Francis, 1928).

An article that captures the common conceptions of assessment length in the workplace is D. A. Waldman, L. E. Atwater, and D. Antioni, "Has 360 Feedback Gone Amok?" *The Academy of Management Executive,* 12 (1998): 86–94.

For more on the typical length of psychological assessments, see Lee J. Cronbach and Paul E. Meehl, "Construct Validity in Psychological Tests," *Psychological Bulletin,* 52 (1955): 281–302. G. W. Morris and M. A. Lo Verde, "Consortium Surveys," in P. Rosenfeld, J. E. Edwards, and M. D. Thomas, eds., *Improving Organizational Surveys: New Directions, Methods, and Applications* (Newbury Park, CA: Sage, 1993): 122–142; and A. Furnham, *The Psychology of Behaviour at Work* (Sussex, England: Psychologist Press, 1997).

On the length of an assessment required for adequate validity, see P. B. Sheatsley, "Questionnaire Construction and Item Writing," in P. H. Rossi, J. D. Wright, and A. B. Anderson, eds., *Handbook of Survey Research* (San Diego: Academic Press, 1983), 195–230.

For the psychometric properties of one of the most valid and widely used assessments, which also happens to have fewer than thirty questions, see A. T. Beck, W. Y. Rial, and K. Rickets. "Short Form of Depression Inventory: Cross-Validation," *Psychological-Reports,* 34, 3 (1974): 1184–1186; and A. T. Beck, R. A. Steer, and M. G. Garbin, "Psychometric Properties of the Beck Depression Inventory: Twenty-five Years of Evaluation," *Clinical Psychology Review,* 8, 1 (1988): 77–100.

On common methods for assessing personality, see D. J. Pittenger, "Measuring the MBTI and Coming Up Short," *Journal of Career Planning & Placement,* Fall 1993. R. R. McCrae and P. T. Costa, "Validation of the Five-Factor Model of Personality Across Instruments and Observers," *Journal of Personality and Social Psychology,* 52 (1987): 81–90.

Appendix B: Behind the Scenes of the TalentSmart Study

In 1904, the French minister of education, Alfred Binet, developed the first intelligence test, which he used to separate stellar students from "lazy" ones. The test had thirty questions, and scores were termed "mental age." A Stanford psychologist, Lewis Terman, coined the term "IQ" in 1914. He developed a new version of the test that was eventually used by the U.S. Army to determine the quality of World War I recruits. An excellent review of this series of events is found in Raymond Fancher's *The Intelligence Men: Makers of the IQ Controversy* (New York: Norton, 1985).

The recognition that something was missing from measures of intelligence was first described as "social intelligence" by E. L. Thorndike's "Intelligence and Its Uses," *Harper's,* 140 (1920): 227–335.

For more on the inability to predict IQ, EQ, and personality and the lack of correlation among these qualities, see Melissa Graves, "Emotional Intelligence, General Intelligence, and Personality: Assessing the Construct Validity of an Emotional Intelligence Test Using Structural Equation Modeling" (unpublished doctoral dissertation, San Diego, California School of Professional Psychology, 1999).

The first study to use the term "emotional intelligence" was a doctoral dissertation by W. L. Payne, "A Study of Emotion: Developing Emotional Intelligence: Self-Integration; Relating to Fear, Pain and Desire" (Cincinnati, The Union Institute, 1988).

For the poor ability of IQ to predict success in life, and the muted impact of measuring and using people's cognitive intelligence as a means of helping them learn and improve, see George Vaillant, *Adaptation to Life* (Boston: Little, Brown, 1977), and Howard Gardner, *Frames of Mind: The Theory of Multiple Intelligences* (New York: Basic Books, 1993).

The emotional intelligence model described here has four parts (self-awareness, self-management, social awareness, and relationship management) with self-awareness as the first critical component. The model was developed by Daniel Goleman, and it is by far the most widely utilized. For more, see Daniel Goleman, Richard Boyatzis, and Annie McKee, *Primal Leadership: Realizing the Power of Emotional Intelligence* (Boston: Harvard Business School Press, 2002).

For more on the Emotional Intelligence Appraisal, see Travis Bradberry and Jean Greaves, *The Emotional Intelligence Quick Book: Everything You Need to Know to Put Your EQ to Work* (New York: Simon & Schuster, 2005).

For more on prefixes for binary multiples, see http://physics.nist.gov/cuu/Units/binary.html.

On face validity, see Robert F. Bornstein, "Face Validity in Psychological Assessment: Implications for a Unified Model of Validity," *American Psychologist,* 51 (1996): 983–984.

For more on the importance of outcome-related measures of workplace performance, see L. E. Atwater and F. J. Yammarino, "Does Self–Other Agreement on Leadership Perceptions Moderate the Validity of Leadership and Performance Predictors?" *Personnel Psychology,* 45 (1992): 141–155.

For a discussion of power, see Jacob Cohen, *Statistical Power Analysis for the Behavioral Sciences,* 2nd ed. (Hillsdale, NJ: Erlbaum, 1988).

On the use of a scree plot to determine the factor solution of an assessment, see R. Catell, "The Scree Test for Number of Factors," *Multivariate Behavioral Research,* 1 (1966): 245–276.

On the use of Z scores set to a value above 1.96 or below −1.96 to assess significance of correlation comparisons, see Julie Paillant, *SPSS Survival Manual: A Step by Step Guide to Data Analysis Using SPSS for Windows (Version 10)* (Maidenhead, England: Open University Press, 2001).

On the use of Varimax Rotation and Kaiser Normalization, see H. Kaiser, "A Second Generation Little Jiffy," *Psychometrika,* 35 (1970): 401–415.

For a discussion of the Miller and Cardy job performance measure, see J. S. Miller and R. L. Cardy, "Self-Monitoring and Performance Appraisal: Rating Outcomes in Project Teams," *Journal of Organizational Behavior,* 21 (2000): 609–626; N. T. Duarte, J. R. Goodson, and N. R. Klich, "Effects of the Dyadic Quality and Duration on Performance Appraisal," *Academy of Management Journal* 37 (1994): 499–521; T. E. Becker, R. S. Billings, D. M. Eveleth, and N. L. Gilbert, "Foci and Bases of Employee Commitment: Implications for Job Performance," *Academy of Management Journal* 39 (1996): 464–482; and M. Freese, W. Kring, A. Soose, and J. Zempel, "Personal Initiative at Work: Differences Between East and West Germany," *Academy of Management Journal,* 39 (1996): 37–63.

Index